Land of Our Lady Series

Founders of Freedom
by
Sister M. Benedict Joseph, S.N.J.M.
Los Angeles, Calif.

Bearers of Freedom
by
Sister M. Veronica, S.P.B.V.
Central Falls, R. I.

Leaders of Freedom
by
Sister M. Clarita, O.P.
Watertown, Mass.

Challenge of Freedom
by
Sister M. Theresine, S.N.D.
Cleveland, Ohio

Guardian of Freedom
by
Sister M. Augusta, H.H.M.
Akron, Ohio

THE NEUMANN PRESS

Our Lady
of
Guadalupe

Pray for us

PRAYER

OUR Lady of Guadalupe, mystical rose, make intercession for Holy Church, protect the Sovereign Pontiff, help all those who invoke thee in their necessities, and since thou art the ever Virgin Mary and Mother of the true God, obtain for us from thy most holy Son the grace of keeping our faith, sweet hope in the midst of the bitterness of life, burning charity and the precious gift of final perseverance.

(Indulgence of 500 days. S.P. Ap., April 29, 1935)

Land of Our Lady Series

Bearers
of
Freedom

by Sister M. Veronica, S.P.B.V.

EDITOR-IN-CHIEF:
Rev. Timothy F. O'Leary, Ph.D.
Assistant Superintendent of Schools
Archdiocese of Boston

ASSISTANT EDITOR-IN-CHIEF:
Sister M. Veronica, S.P.B.V.

CO-EDITORS:
Rt. Rev. Clarence E. Elwell, Ph.D.
Superintendent of Schools
Diocese of Cleveland

Rev. Patrick J. Roche, Ph.D.
Assistant Superintendent of Schools
Archdiocese of Los Angeles

REPUBLISHED BY
THE NEUMANN PRESS
LONG PRAIRIE, MINNESOTA

BY SPECIAL ARRANGEMENT WITH
BENZIGER PUBLISHING COMPANY
NEW YORK, CINCINNATI, CHICAGO, BOSTON, SAN FRANCISCO

Nihil Obstat:

JOHN M. A. FEARNS, S.T.D.,
Censor Librorum.

Imprimatur:

† FRANCIS CARDINAL SPELLMAN,
Archbishop of New York.

July 15, 1952.

ISBN 0-911845-54-2
THIS 1997 EDITION IS PUBLISHED THROUGH SPECIAL ARRANGEMENT WITH
BENZIGER PUBLISHING COMPANY BY
THE NEUMANN PRESS
LONG PRAIRIE, MINNESOTA

Editors' Preface

The "Land of Our Lady" Series presents an accurate historical account of our nation's history as Divine Providence has unfolded it to us. Its pages reveal the story of the Catholic Church in the development of the land dedicated to the Immaculate Conception of the Blessed Mother of God.

This series is intended to give boys and girls a practical realization of the Christian philosophy of life by applying correctly the principles of Christian social living to the historical content.

The compilers of these texts have successfully endeavored to keep the vocabulary of each textbook within the range of the pupils' speaking vocabulary at each grade level. Narrative form is retained throughout the Series in the presentation of content.

While the Series is based upon a definitely factual background of history, the factual data is clarified by as lucid an explanation of events as possible, and a clear description of the contents of the concepts involved.

The maps, charts, and other illustrative material accompanying the textual material are devoted solely to the simplifying of the historical data for the pupils and the clarification of the text itself.

The content is psychologically woven into *units* of subject matter, each unit comprising a portion of history, which, in itself, is a related whole. Each unit, in turn, is broken down into two or more chapters.

For the greater benefit of the teacher, each unit in the text is outined, and this outline is followed by a preview of each unit.

Activities are found at the end of each chapter as well as at the end of each unit. The Mastery Tests at the end of each unit are a final check-up for the pupils on the essentials of that unit.

We earnestly hope that this Series will be productive of much good and inspire young Catholic American boys and girls with a greater realization of the priceless value of being good Catholics and, therefore, good citizens in this glorious Land of Our Lady.

THE EDITORS.

Contents

UNIT ONE

GOD'S GIFT—AMERICA

UNIT TWO

WITH SADDLES AND SANDALS

UNIT THREE

FOR SOULS AND SABLES

UNIT FOUR
HOMEMAKERS ALL

UNIT FIVE
ROUNDING OUT THIRTEEN

UNIT SIX
FRENCH LANDS IN ENGLISH HANDS

FOREWORD

The publication of the "Land of Our Lady" Series marks a notable advancement in the field of history textbooks for Catholic elementary schools. The Series fulfills very effectively the need for history textbooks that are devoid of secularistic and materialistic tendencies and based on the sound principles of Christianity and therefore, a Christian philosophy of history.

This Series includes not only the factual data that comprise the history of America as a nation, but it incorporates also those elements of American Catholic history that can be assimilated by pupils of the elementary school level. The growth and development of the Catholic Church in the United States parallels the content of American history in each textbook of the Series.

The greatest contribution of these texts to the training and schooling of young American Catholic boys and girls is the manner in which Christian social principles are woven in the texts. As the various events of history are taken up for study, the textbooks point out the positive or negative correlation of the factual data to the principles of Christian social living.

We are grateful to the firm of Benziger Brothers, and to the competent Board of Editors and Authors for the task they have successfully accomplished in producing this American Catholic Series, "Land of Our Lady."

RT. REV. FREDERICK G. HOCHWALT, PH.D.
SECRETARY GENERAL, N.C.E.A.

Our Lady of Pompeii

Pray for us

PRAYER

Mary, most holy Virgin and Queen of Martyrs, accept the sincere homage of my filial affection. Into thy heart, pierced by so many swords, do thou welcome my poor soul. Receive it as the companion of thy sorrows at the foot of the Cross, on which Jesus died for the redemption of the world. With thee, O sorrowful Virgin, I will gladly suffer all trials contradictions, and infirmities which it shall please our Lord to send me. I offer them all to thee in memory of thy sorrows, so that every thought of my mind, and every beat of my heart may be an act of compassion and of love for thee. And do thou, sweet Mother, have pity on me, reconcile me to thy divine Son Jesus, keep me in His grace and assist me in my last agony, so that I may be able to meet thee in heaven and sing thy glories. Amen.

(Indulgence of 500 days (S. C. Ind., Mar. 20, 1887; S. P. Ap., May 19, 1934 and June 18, 1949).

UNIT ONE

GOD'S GIFT—AMERICA!

CHAPTER I—SAILORS, SILKS, AND TRADERS

The Northmen sought new lands.

The Christian Northmen visited the shores of America.

Christians of Europe made pilgrimages to the Holy Land.

The Mohammedans captured the Holy Land.

The Crusades were started to save the Holy Land.

Trade with the East began at the time of the Crusades.

Marco Polo visited the East.

Marco Polo wrote about his travels.

The art of printing helped to spread knowledge.

Trade routes were closed after the fall of of Constantinople.

Men began to seek new ways of getting to the East.

CHAPTER II — A NEW ROUTE TO INDIA

Prince Henry trained his sailors to become good navigators.

Dias discovered the Cape of Good Hope at the southern tip of Africa.

Da Gama found a route to India by way of the Atlantic Ocean.

CHAPTER III — GREATER THAN GOLD

Columbus planned to reach the East by sailing West.

Columbus asked help from Portugal.

The Portuguese King refused to help Columbus.

Columbus was befriended by the Franciscan Fathers.

Columbus was ready to seek help from France.

Columbus was given help by Spain.

Columbus discovered a great continent that lay between Europe and the Indies.

Columbus made several voyages to the New World.

The enemies of Columbus were cruel to him.

Columbus died alone, poor, and forsaken.

The land Columbus discovered was called America.

Through Columbus God gave the world a new land.

UNIT ONE

GOD'S GIFT — AMERICA!

America, Land of Freedom. We are fortunate to be living in this great land. Here the people enjoy many wonderful rights and privileges. We should be most grateful to Almighty God for these blessings. Do you ever thank Him for giving us this glorious land, which we call Amrica?

For thousands and thousands of years Indians had been living in our land. Of course, it was their land then. They passed their time each day in the search for food, chiefly by hunting and fishing. The Indians never met people of other lands.

People from other countries did not know that America existed. The first ones to come to its shores were the Northmen, who were Christians. This happened about one thousand years after the birth of Christ, Our Saviour.

The Northmen stayed awhile and then returned to their own country. Their visit was soon forgotten.

Then came the year 1492. One pleasant day in October, three Spanish ships landed at an island where some Indians lived. A brave captain led his men to shore. Here they knelt to thank God for His goodness to them.

These Spaniards thought they had reached the   **13**

rich lands of the East. But this land was not the Indies. It was land that lay between Spain and the Indies. It was our own America!

God plans all things well. He planned that the Spaniards should find this new land. He planned that they should bring with them the Christian religion. God planned that Columbus, their leader, should give His gift to the world, His gift of AMERICA, land of freedom!

God's Gift. We shall learn in this book that the early discoverers and explorers of America were Catholics.

We shall learn how the Catholic faith was brought to America by these explorers, who were usually accompanied by missionaries.

The missionaries accompanied the explorers to bring the teachings of our holy faith to the Indians who lived here.

Thus, from very early times the Catholic faith was a part of America. This is great heritage.

We say that America is a land of freedom. This means that in this land of ours we are allowed to do what is right. No one may force us to do what is wrong.

The freedom we enjoy today is based upon the teaching of the Catholic Church.

As we read this first unit we shall learn about the beginnings of this land of freedom. We shall see how Columbus planted the cross on the shores

of the New World, and claimed this land.

CHAPTER I

SAILORS, SILKS, AND TRADERS

Looking Over the Chapter. Long ago in the North of Europe there lived a whole nation of sailors. These sailors spent days and days at sea, visiting distant lands, and discovering new ones.

On one of these trips, they came upon a land which they called Vinland. After a short visit, they sailed away again. Vinland was really a part of our own great land, America.

Before the Crusades, people in Europe knew very little about the way people lived in Asia. But when the Crusaders came back from the East, they brought back to Europe some of the new and beautiful goods of the East. Some of these articles were silks, satins, and spices.

Now the people in Europe wanted more of these wonderful things. So their traders, or merchants, went to the East to get them. This trade with the East was going along well until the trade routes to the East were cut off.

A new route was needed. The search began for a water route to the East. In their search for a **15** water route, the people in Europe were working out God's plan for the world.

When you have read this chapter, you will know the complete story of sailors, silks, and traders. It tells the things that happened in Europe before the search for a new route began.

A NATION OF SAILORS

DENMARK, Norway, and Sweden are in the North of Europe. Can you find them on the map? A very brave people called Northmen lived there. Sometimes the pirate seamen among the Northmen are called Vikings, which means "sea-warriors."

The soil of these countries was very poor and unsuitable for farming. However, the Northmen succeeded in raising a few crops by the coast. They made their living by hunting and fishing.

The Northmen learned to build ships which were strong enough to stand storms at sea. At the front of these long, black ships with huge sails was carved the head of a monster. Each ship was equipped with ten to twenty oars. The Northmen often went on long fishing trips on the ocean, far to the west of their native land.

Later, the Northmen changed their manner of making a living. They began to attack the sea-coast towns of Britain and Gaul. They raided the homes of the people, and put women and children to death. They became a nation of pirates.

16

Seeking New Lands. About 850 A.D. the Northmen discovered Iceland far to the west of Norway and established a colony there. A colony is a group of persons living in another land, but governed by the people of their own land.

A long time afterwards, a Northman named Eric the Red committed a murder in his village in Norway. The people in his village were very angry at him for this deed. He left Norway and went to Iceland to live.

But after a short time in Iceland, he boarded his ship and set sail farther west through unknown waters. He discovered a large island which he called Greenland.

Eric the Red hoped that people from Iceland would want to live on this land. Several shiploads of colonists from Iceland went to Greenland to live. These colonists carried on trade with their native land.

A Great Discovery. Eric the Red had two sons. The more famous one was called Leif Ericson. Leif (leaf) grew tired of the quiet life in the Greenland colony. One day he set out to visit Norway, the native land of his father.

When Leif reached Norway, he found that the Northmen there had given up their false gods and had become Christians. Leif also became a Christian. A Christian is one who follows the teachings of Christ. Then the King of Norway asked Leif Ericson to return to Greenland and tell the 17 colonists there about Christianity. Christianity means the religion of Christians.

Leif set sail for Greenland about the year 1000 A.D. The Northmen were very good sailors. They did not have a single map or chart. They steered their boats by the sun, moon and stars.

Sometimes at sea in bad weather, they could not even see the sun, moon, or stars. The Northmen must have put their trust in God and Mary. Soon after Leif and his men passed Iceland they ran into a terrible storm. The ship almost sank beneath the huge waves, and the sails were torn by the strong wind.

The sturdy ship was driven far from Greenland. When the storm had passed, the shores of a new land appeared. After this discovery, Leif Ericson became known as Leif the Lucky.

Vinland and America. The place where Leif Ericson's crew landed was somewhere on the eastern shore of our America. Many people think it was Nova Scotia or Labrador. Others think is was some part of New England. Of course this land was not called America then.

The Northmen found clusters and clusters of wild grapes on the spot where they landed. Because of this, Leif Ericson called it Vinland. In English we would say "Vine-land."

The Northmen built log cabins and spent the winter in Vinland. When spring came they returned to Greenland, their boats laden with grapes.

These Northmen were the first Christians to come to America. They were also the first to bring Christianity to the Indians.

Three years later, Leif Ericson's brother tried to start a colony in Vinland. But the little group of Northmen became discouraged. They deserted the land because the Indians, who were much more numerous than they, frequently attacked them. After this attempt, the Northmen never returned to Vinland.

If the Northmen had claimed Vinland as theirs, we would say they had discovered America.

The Northmen and their deeds were almost forgotten because they did not keep a record of their voyages. After a long time, someone wrote down stories that were told about the Northmen. We call these stories "sagas." It is the word the Northmen used for long tales of bravery.

After the Northmen had visited America, almost five hundred years passed before anyone else sailed West across the Atlantic Ocean.

CRUSADERS ON THE MARCH

Visiting the Holy Land. Christ Our Saviour lived on this earth for thirty-three years. He lived in a country called Palestine. Palestine is called the Holy Land because it was the land of the Jews, God's chosen people. When Christ came to earth to redeem all men, He lived there. This made the land still more holy. Look at the map and see if you can find Palestine.

The Apostles began to preach the Gospel of Christ after the Holy Ghost came and strengthened them. Christianity spread throughout the countries of Europe.

Some of the Christians of Europe decided to visit the Holy Places in Palestine, where Christ suffered and died. These journeys to the Holy Land were called *pilgrimages*. They were long and tiresome for the Christians. However, they gladly suffered the fatigue and hardships of the journey for the love of Christ. You too, can show God how much you love Him by offering Him

your sacrifices.

The Strange Religion of Mohammed. In the year 571 A.D. a man named Mohammed (mo-ham'-ed) was born in Arabia. Mohammed was a trader, and used to go on long journeys through the desert-lands. In these journeys, he met many Jews and Christians. From them he learned many things about their religions. Mohammed began to think more and more about these things. He then decided to make up a religion of his own.

Mohammed said he was a prophet and Allah was his God. He meant the same God we believe in, the one true God. His followers are called Moslems. That means "people who do God's will." They call their religion "Islam." But we call them by the name of their founder. We call them "Mohammedans."

Mohammed wrote his ideas in a book called the Koran. Some of his ideas are really true, but many others are strange and false. Even now, the Koran is just as important to the Mohammedans as the Bible is to the Christians.

Mohammed taught his followers that if they should die fighting those who would not accept his religion, they would go straight to heaven. This is an example of the bad advice he gave his followers. We Christians have the good, holy teaching of Christ to help us at all times.

Holy Land in Danger. After Mohammed died, his followers carried his religion into the countries of Asia. The Arabs were ruling the Holy Land at this time. They were Mohammedans. About the year 1071, the Turks captured the Holy Land from the Arabs.

These Turks were also Mohammedans, and were very unfriendly towards the Christians.

The Turks caused great damage in Palestine. They destroyed the churches of the Christians, and ruined the holy places. They then built their own temples, which they called *mosques* (mosks). They robbed and tortured the Christians who made pilgrimages to Palestine. Sometimes they even put them to death.

When the Christians in Europe heard that the Turks had captured the Holy Land, they were very sad. They knew they could no longer make pilgrimages to the Holy Land. It would be too dangerous to go there.

War Begins. The Holy Father at that time was Pope Urban II. He wanted the Holy Land to be rescued from the Mohammedans. He asked the Christians of Europe to raise an army to fight the Mohammedans and save the holy places.

Immediately, the Christians obeyed the Pope and started to raise a great army. This war to save the Holy Land was called a *Crusade*. Those who fought in this war were called *Crusaders*.

In 1095, a large army of Crusaders left for the Holy Land. This was the first Crusade. The watchword of the Crusaders was "God wills it." This was written on their flags and banners.

Not all the Crusaders were holy people. Some of them did not become Crusaders out of love for God or to do His holy will. Some went to the East to become wealthy, not to save the holy places.

In all, there were ten Crusades. Still, the Christians did not save the Holy Land. The Christians

won some battles against the Turks, but lost many others.

SILKS, SATINS, AND CINNAMON

New Ways of Living. Before the Crusades, people in Europe did not know how the people in Asia lived. When the Crusaders returned, they told wonderful stories about the rich lands of the Orient, as the eastern countries are called. They 23 showed their friends some of the products of the East. There were spices such as cloves, nutmeg, pepper, and cinnamon.

Other articles that came from the East were sparkling diamonds, rubies, and other precious stones, and sweet perfumes.

The Crusaders also brought back many products to make their clothes and homes more beautiful. They brought yards and yards of silk and satin cloth. There were also beautiful rugs and tapestries, and richly-colored material for curtains and drapes.

The Crusaders bought many of these products in the shops of Constantinople and other cities through which they passed. But these things really came from lands still farther away. They were produced in distant lands called the *Indies.* Today we call these lands India, China, and Japan.

THE TRADERS OF ITALY

MANY of the people in Europe were pleased with all the fine things the Crusaders brought home. These people wanted more spices, more jewels, more rugs and carpets. In exchange for the rich goods of the East, Europe sent wool, tin, leather, and wheat to the Orient. Trade with the East began during the days of the Crusades.

Rivals in Trade. Two cities in Italy, Venice (ven'-iss) and Genoa (jen'-o-a), had fine harbors. Find them on your map. The traders, or merchants, in these cities sent their ships to Eastern ports. At these ports they built storehouses. The storehouses were to hold the rich goods that the merchants had bought in the East.

When their ships arrived from Italy, they filled them with the precious articles from the storehouses.

One famous port of trade was Constantinople, on the Black Sea. This was one of the largest and most beautiful cities in the world. It had many churches and palaces.

When the ships came back to Italy, people in all other parts of Europe bought these articles from the merchants in Venice and Genoa. This trade made the merchants of these cities wealthy.

The cities themselves became rich and powerful. Each tried to do better than the other.

Before long the two cities became enemies and started to wage war. We shall see later how a great traveler was imprisoned because of these wars between the two cities.

PATHS OF TRADE

The Camel Parade. In those days there were three famous routes to the Far East. If you were a merchant in those days, you would have used one of these three routes.

If you had chosen the first route, you would follow the Northern Route, which led to China, or Cathay (ka-thay'). When you reached the port of Constantinople, you would ride a big camel. **25**

You would see hundreds and hundreds of camels on this route. A group of merchants traveling with their camels is called a *caravan*.

Mostly by Water. The Southern Route was mostly by water. Ships from Italy would land at towns on the southern shore of the Mediterranean Sea. The camels would carry the cargoes from the ships across the Isthmus of Suez (soo'-ez) to the

Red Sea. Find on your classroom map the narrow strip of land called the Isthmus of Suez.

Then the travelers and their goods sailed down the Red Sea to the land of Cathay.

The Third Route. The third route lay halfway between the Northern and Southern Routes, and was called the Middle Route. The merchants liked this one best, because there were many large cities along the way where they could exchange their goods. When they came to the Persian Gulf, they would sail to the Indian Ocean. Then they would sail to India. Can you trace the trade routes on your map?

Dangers of the Trade Routes. The journeys to the East were hard for the merchants. The return journeys were even more dangerous. The caravans journeyed along, loaded with goods worth thousands and thousands of dollars. Often robbers would attack the caravans and steal the precious loads, and many of the drivers would be killed. **27**

THE most famous traveler to the East was a young man from Venice. His name was Marco Polo.

While he was still very young, Marco Polo's father and uncle visited Cathay, or China. They went to the court of the great Kublai Khan (koo'-bli-con), who was Emperor of China.

The emperor was very kind to them, and wanted them to tell him more about Europe. They stayed seventeen years in Cathay. Then they returned to Venice.

In China. Shortly after they returned to Venice, they set out again for Cathay. This time they took Marco with them. It took them four years to reach Cathay. How do you think they traveled?

The great Kublai Khan liked Marco Polo very much. He made him his special messenger to the most distant parts of his kingdom. Marco Polo lived in this land for twenty years. He often desired to return to Venice, but Kublai Khan was so pleased with him that he would not allow him to leave China.

MISSIONARIES TO CHINA

FINALLY, Kublai Khan allowed Marco Polo to return to Europe with his father and uncle. When they were leaving Cathay, Kublai Khan gave them a message for the Pope. In this message Kublai

Khan asked the Pope to send some missionaries to Cathay.

Franciscan missionaries then went to China. The emperor received them with great kindness. He did not become a Christian, nor did many of his people. Yet the missionaries did what they could to spread the Kingdom of God in this land.

Later, when these missionaries returned to Europe, they gave the people much valuable information about the distant lands of the Orient.

TALES OF A CAPTURED TRAVELER

THE people of Venice did not recognize the Polo travelers when they returned to their own land. Their clothes were so old and shabby that people thought they were beggars.

But then, the surprise came. The beggars began to rip open the seams of their old clothes. The most dazzling jewels, diamonds, and precious stones fell from the clothes of the ragged beggars.

Since the Polos were really wealthy, why do you think they came back to Venice dressed in old clothes?

Days in Prison. Soon after the Polos returned, war broke out between Venice and Genoa. Marco Polo was captured and taken to a prison in Genoa.

While he was in prison, Marco Polo told many stories to the other prisoners. He told them of the wonderful land of Cathay, and of its riches. People say he told "tall tales." He made the land appear far more wealthy than it really was.

A Book of Travels. While Marco Polo was in prison, he began to write about the riches he had seen in Cathay and other lands of the Indies. He called his book "The Travels of Marco Polo."

In those days, books had to be copied by hand. Everyone knew about Marco Polo's book. Only a few had a chance to read it, because there were so few copies.

The Printing Press. Many years later, about the year 1450, printing from movable type was invented. After this, many copies could be made on a printing press.

The first book to be printed was the Holy Bible. It was in the Latin language. One of the first of these Catholic Bibles is in a library in Washington, D. C. Can you guess what was printed next? It was "The Travels of Marco Polo."

Popular Book. Soon everyone was reading the famous book about Cathay. It became, next to the Holy Bible, the most popular book of the day.

More than ever before, the people of Europe wanted the wealth of the East, which was described in Marco Polo's book. They felt they could not do without it. Trade with the East increased after this book was printed.

CAPTURE OF CONSTANTINOPLE

Danger Ahead. For quite a while after the Crusades, the merchants of Venice and Genoa made plenty of money by trading with the East. The people of Europe were very pleased with their new ways of living. They felt they could never again get along without the precious products of the East.

After about two hundred years a savage group of Turks began to invade lands in the East. The great city of Constantinople was in danger of attack.

The Fall of a Great City. Finally the Turks attacked the beautiful city of Constantinople. A great battle was fought. After fifty-three days of fighting, Constantinople fell. It was the year 1453.

The Turks made Constantinople the center of their great Turkish kingdom. The beautiful churches of the Christians became mosques where the Turks went to pray.

Trade Routes Cut Off. The capture of Constantinople by the Turks was a great misfortune for the merchants of Venice and Genoa. The Northern Route to Cathay was no longer safe. Few merchants dared to travel that route. They used the other two trade routes. But even these became daily more dangerous.

God has given every human being the right to life and property. The Turks had no regard for the life or property of others. They killed many innocent people. They built fleets of ships which robbed all other ships on the Mediterranean Sea.

Trade routes were cut off. There would be no more riches for Europe. Merchants of Venice and Genoa lost all their wealth.

Imagine that on your way home from school today you met a sign which read, "Road Closed." What would you do? Wouldn't you take another road home? Certainly.

But the people of Europe did not know of any other route to the Indies. The only routes they knew were the three trade routes, and these were now closed to them.

The people still wanted the wealth of the East for themselves. They wanted more spices, more jewels, more rugs and carpets. They decided to look for another route to the East. They wanted a safe water route.

God draws good out of everything. In their greed for riches, without their thinking about it, the people of Europe were working out God's plan.

God's plan was that a new world be discovered. He wanted more and more people in the world to know about Him and His Church.

The people of Europe wanted to find a new way to the East. But most of them only wanted to do this to make it easier to get riches and goods.

Word Study

Marco Polo	pilgrimage	spices	Koran
trade routes	merchants	Crusade	sagas
Kublai Khan	Urban II	mosques	Orient
Mohammedans	Northmen	caravans	Indies
Christianity	tapestries		

Testing Your Learning

1. Draw a line six inches long on your paper. At the beginning of the line write the date of the beginning of the Crusades; at the center of the line place the date when Marco Polo visited China; at the end of the line write the date of the fall of Constantinople. Afterwards you may illustrate this time-line.

2. Try to answer the following questions. If you are not able to do so, you may reread the chapter. The answers are within the chapter, but they are "hidden," that is, they are written in different words than those which are used here.

    a. Why do we study the Crusades in a story of trade with the East?

    b. Why is the invention of printing important to this story?

    c. Why is Marco Polo's trip to the East important?

    d. Why did Venice and Genoa alone trade with the East?

    e. How did the goods of the East reach Europe?

    f. How did the fall of Constantinople bring about the closing of the trade routes?

    g. Why do we not call the Northmen discoverers of America?

3. Do people ever join Crusades today. Do you know any such Crusades?

4. Prepare to discuss the following question with your classmates: "Why did the people of Europe begin to look for an all-water route to the East after the land routes were closed?"

5. Trace the trade routes on your map. Find Constantinople, Genoa, Venice, Indian Ocean, Cathay. **33**

CHAPTER II

A NEW ROUTE TO INDIA

Looking Over the Chapter. The merchants of Italy wanted to carry on trade with the East. After the trade routes to the East were cut off, they wanted to find a new, all-water route to India.

Many people thought such a route was impossible. A young, daring prince of Portugal, however, believed it could be found. He himself trained his sailors. After they were trained he sent them out upon the high seas.

On the nearby waters of the Atlantic, the sailors set out to find India. No one knew how far to the south the Atlantic Ocean extended. Yet each day the sailors went farther away from their homeland. South, south, south!

Many sailors were afraid and turned back. Yet each crew of sailors sailed a little farther south than the others before them.

What was the great secret of the sea? Where did these sailors land? In this chapter, we shall find out for ourselves the answers to the questions.

The Plans of a Prince. Portugal was the first country to begin the search for a water route to India. Portugal is a small country west of Spain, bordering on the Atlantic Ocean.

The king of this land had five sons, one of whom was named Henry. Prince Henry was different from his brothers. Instead of enjoying the life at Court, he wanted to travel. He fought in battle like an ordinary soldier, and as a young sailor he visited many countries.

Because he did so much traveling on ocean **35**

voyages, people called him "Prince Henry the Navigator."

Now, Prince Henry had one great ambition. He wanted to find an all-water route to India, so that Portugal could obtain the gold and riches of the East. He also wanted to bring Christianity to the natives of India.

But Prince Henry knew that Portugal had few sailors, and they were not trained to sail the mighty ocean. They did not know half as much about the seas as the Northmen had learned. They still believed in a terrible "Sea of Darkness" that went all the way round the earth at the outside edges.

Sailors Go to School. What did Prince Henry do? He started a school in his palace by the sea. Could you have gone to Prince Henry's school? Oh, no! for this was a school for sailors.

In Prince Henry's palace, many husky sailors studied. They studied maps, charts, and books about sea-voyages. They spent long, long hours learning more and more about the size of the world. They would go up into Prince Henry's look-out tower to study the sun, or the moon and the stars at night.

Sailors Study Inventions. Prince Henry taught his sailors how to use the compass. The Chinese invented the compass, but people in Europe did not know about it until the time of the Crusades. This marvelous invention was a piece of steel or iron, which always pointed North. By using a compass, the sailors could tell the direction their ship was going. Did you ever magnetize a needle and float it on water to make a compass?

Another great invention was the astrolabe. The astrolabe told the sailors the position of the sun or stars. In this way they could tell how far north or south of the equator their ship was located. Today sailors use another instrument, called a "sextant." The sextant has taken the place of the astrolabe.

Inventions like the compass and the astrolabe helped the Portuguese to become better sailors. God had given them the knowledge of these wonderful instruments.

All inventions had their first beginning in the mind of Almighty God. They work so well only because He put such perfect order in the stars and planets of the beautiful sky.

ROUNDING THE CAPE

Ship Ahoy! At last Prince Henry's sailors were ready for their daring adventures.

In those days, people knew very little about the Atlantic Ocean. No one knew how far south of Portugal it extended. All sailors thought that large sea-animals lived in the ocean. The sailors were afraid these animals would devour them if they sailed far out to sea. That is why the first seamen from Prince Henry's school always sailed in sight of land. They steered their tiny ships close to the 37 shore as they went south on the waters of the great Atlantic.

These sailors would travel for a while, then the mighty sea would frighten them. Before long, they were home again in Prince Henry's seaside palace.

Now it was time for the sailors who studied in Prince Henry's school to prove that they had learned their lessons well. Each group traveled farther and farther.

Each daring captain, with his crew, went a little farther south than the one before him. One came home to tell Prince Henry that the coast of Africa turned east. Today we call this the Gold Coast. Can you find it on your map?

Another sailor told Prince Henry that the land turned south again beyond the Gold Coast. This was valuable information to Prince Henry, but he was not satisfied. He wanted his sailors to continue their journey on the Atlantic until they should find a new route to India.

At this time, Prince Henry the Navigator, friend of sailors, died. Other great sailors, whom he had trained in his school, continued his work.

A High Wind Leads to a Great Discovery. In 1488, Bartholomew Dias (deé-as), a great sailor, sailed past the Gold Coast. He went farther south along the coast than the others before him had gone. He always stayed in sight of land. He took no risk roaming far away from the coast.

A great wind blew from the north. It was strong and swift. Bartholomew and his crew were at the mercy of the wind. Farther and farther south the wind drove their frail vessel.

Could they see the coast line now? No; the storm was too heavy. They thought they would be lost.

Finally, the storm passed. Dias looked to the north, the south, the east, the west. There was no land in sight. Which way would he turn? If only he could see land again!

He turned his ship towards the east. No land **39**

there. He steered north. There he found land

The land Dias discovered was a cape. He called it the Cape of Storms. Can you tell why?

There was now great rejoicing among the sailors. They knew they had reached the southern tip of Africa.

Dias wanted to sail on until he reached India, but his sailors were afraid to go any farther. Dias had to turn back and sail home to Portugal.

The King of Portugal was happy when he heard the news about the great discovery. He called the new land the Cape of Good Hope. Now there was hope of soon reaching India. Even today it is called by that name. Can you find this cape on your map?

It was a high wind that led Dias to discover the Cape of Good Hope in 1488. God makes use of all things, even a wind, to do good to us, His creatures. Should we not thank Him for His great care of us?

RICHES RARE FOR PORTUGAL

ANOTHER sailor, Vasco da Gama, was determined to reach India. In 1498 he set out, using the same route traveled by Dias as far as the cape.

Da Gama was a skillful sailor. He, too, met great storms. He said he had never before seen such tempests as he met at the tip of Africa. He realized why Dias had called it the Cape of Storms.

India Found by a New Route. After passing the cape safely, Da Gama turned his ship towards the north, then to the east. Within three weeks he had reached the coast of India! While Da Gama was in India, he visited a wealthy prince who lived there. From this prince Da Gama obtained many rich spices, such as ginger, cloves, and nutmeg, and the finest pepper.

On the next page you can see a picture of Da Gama talking to the prince of India. He is telling him about the wonders of Europe, and asking him to trade with the Europeans.

Into the hold of Da Gama's ship went the treasures of India. Now Portugal would have the rich products of the East.

By exploring the Atlantic, sailors of Portugal had found the secret of the sea. They found a new route to India by way of the Atlantic Ocean.

Da Gama Claims the Land. Since Da Gama had succeeded in reaching India, he claimed the land for Portugal.

To show that he claimed the land, he erected a marble pillar. For many years after his voyage, there were Portugese settlements on the coast of India at places where Da Gama had landed.

It was one of these places that Saint Francis Xavier later visited on his way to China. The Portuguese built many churches and taught the Indian people about Christ and our holy faith.

Results of Da Gama's Voyage. Da Gama and his men not only found a new route to India, they also brought many riches to Portugal.

This made Portugal a very wealthy nation. It was then able to send many other sailors and explorers to distant places on the earth.

We shall see later in this book how the Portuguese made explorations in what later became our own land, the United States of America.

A Little Quiz

Write a sentence about each of the words: Constantinople, Crusades, Prince Henry, Dias, compass.

Word Study

lookout tower	compass	sextant
astrolabe	invention	devour
extended	instrument	equator

CHAPTER III

GREATER THAN GOLD

The Search for Gold. In 1498, the Portuguese found a new route to India. Then Portugal became a rich country. Can you tell why?

Another country in Europe was interested in the marvelous riches of the East. It also sought an all-water route to the East. That country was Spain.

But God had other plans for the people of Spain. They did not reach the Indies.

Read in this chapter the story of Spain's search for gold. You will want to know how it ended. You will want to know what it means when you read that the Spaniards found something "greater than gold."

A PLAN TO REACH THE INDIES

The Boy of Genoa. About five hundred years ago, in the beautiful town of Genoa, Italy, Christopher Columbus was born.

You know the story of the Saint Christopher, or "Christ-bearer." Christopher was a fitting name for this boy of Genoa. Because of him the 43 knowledge of Christ was to be carried to another land far away.

Christopher was the oldest in a family of four boys and one girl. His father, Dominic, made his living by weaving cloth. Dominic's home was both shop and school, where he taught young boys the weaver's trade. Dominic belonged to the Guild of Clothiers of Genoa. Guilds in those days were somewhat like our unions today. Do you know anyone who belongs to a union?

Christopher and his brother Bartholomew would card the raw wool that their father had bought. Then their mother would spin it into yarn, dye it, and make it ready for the loom. Christopher's father owned two looms, on which he wove the wool into cloth. By selling the cloth, he supported his family.

After school, Christopher would often skip down to the beach or sit on the wharf, watching the strange ships come and go. Here he would listen by the hour to tales of the sea told by the sailors.

The Call of the Ocean. Columbus liked the smooth, white sails and the water's foam. He made up his mind to be a sailor. He was growing up now. He was a tall young man, with red hair and clear, steel-gray eyes.

Near Columbus' home in Genoa, there lived two great noblemen. These men owned many ships. Often they took Columbus on long voyages with them. Young Christopher Columbus visited England on one of these voyages.

Once in a great sea-battle on the Mediterranean Sea, Columbus had to jump overboard to save his life. He held on tightly to a piece of floating wreckage until it brought him safely to shore.

Where do you think he landed? He landed on the shore of Portugal, close to Prince Henry's school by the sea.

Columbus Plans to Sail West. While Columbus was in Portugal, he obtained some maps, which he studied well. He looked upon them as his dearest treasures.

Marco Polo's book had been printed by this time. Columbus read it over and over again. He learned much about the East from this book.

At this time, many people in Europe thought the world was flat. They thought that anyone who sailed too far out on the ocean would fall off the earth.

You know this could not happen, because the earth is round like a ball. There is a strong pull coming from the center of the earth that keeps any such thing from happening.

Columbus knew the earth is round. He had a great plan in his mind which he wanted to carry out. He believed that if he sailed westward on the great Atlantic he would reach the East.

Was Columbus right? Let us try a little experiment and see what happens. Draw a straight line around a ball or an orange, and watch where the line ends. The line runs into the starting point, doesn't it? If you called the beginning of your line West, then half-way around the ball would be the East. The West met the East, did it not?

Then Columbus was right in believing that the West could meet the East. But did Columbus get to the East? Did he carry out his plan? These questions will be good points to talk about after you have read this whole chapter.

DISCOURAGEMENT AND DISAPPOINTMENT

Unkindness of a King. Columbus went to the King of Portugal to ask help for his voyage. This king was named John the Second. He was most unkind to Columbus. He made fun of Columbus because Columbus said he would reach the East by sailing west. At last Columbus became sad and disappointed, and left the King.

The King of Portugal then began to think about Columbus' plan. He secretly called a group of his sailors and told them to explore the Atlantic Ocean to the west. Now these men did not believe in Columbus' plan, so, after a few days on the ocean, they came back to the King. These men told him there were no lands in the west.

When Columbus heard what the Portuguese King had done, he became very angry. He decided to seek help from Spain.

Columbus in Spain. Columbus and his son Diego (dee-ay′-go) set out for Spain. As they entered the town of Palos, Columbus saw the Franciscan Monastery of La Rabida (lah rah′-bee-dah). Here he placed little Diego. He knew the good Franciscan Fathers would take care of him. Franciscans are priests who give themselves to God by following the rules Saint Francis of Assisi laid down.

At the monastery Columbus met Father de Marchena (day mar-chay′-nah) and told him of his plan. This priest encouraged Columbus. He also introduced him to some wealthy people in Palos who could tell him what to do.

These people told Columbus to ask the King and Queen of Spain to help him. Then when he reached the land of the Indies, they said, he should claim it for Spain.

At another time when he visited La Rabida, Columbus met Father Juan Perez (hwan pay'-rayth). Father Perez was a great friend of Queen Isabella. "I shall speak to the Queen for you," Father said.

The Father told Queen Isabella about Columbus' plan to reach the Indies. She said she could not help him at that time because Spain was too busy fighting the Moors. The Moors were followers of Mohammed. They came up into Spain from northern Africa, and overran all of Spain. They were very fierce fighters.

Columbus would not give up. He was discouraged, but he did not change his plans. He decided to seek help from France.

A Fresh Disappointment. Father Perez was sad when he saw Columbus prepare to leave Spain. He sent a letter to the Queen, telling her that Columbus was getting ready to go to France. As quickly as possible, she wrote back, "Come to Court, Father Perez. Encourage Columbus to stay in Spain. I shall soon send for him." She then sent Columbus money to buy a mule so that he could travel to Court.

At last the Queen called Columbus to Court. First, he had to tell his plans to the royal counsellors. The counsellors were men who advised the King and Queen on what to do. These men did not believe that anyone could reach India by sailing west. They advised the King and Queen not to help Columbus.

Columbus had tried and tried, but no one would give him the help he wanted. Seven years passed in this way.

Again Columbus decided to go to France. He saddled his mule and packed his saddlebags. Columbus and his friend Father Perez started for France.

A Message from the Queen! Another friend of Columbus, Luis Santangel (loo'-ees sant'-an-hel), told the Queen that Columbus had left for France. "If he makes a great discovery," he said to the Queen, "it will not be for the glory of Spain. He will claim the land for France."

The Queen made up her mind very quickly. "Even though the wise men here at court do not approve of Columbus," said the good Queen, "I can help him. I shall sell my jewels, if necessary." Luis Santangel said that he, too, would help Columbus to get ships and supplies.

Immediately, the Queen sent a messenger after Columbus. He was four miles outside the city before the messenger overtook him. "Come back, Columbus," said the Queen's messenger. "Come back to Court. The Queen will help you. She will furnish you with ships for your voyage."

Columbus turned back. He hoped that, at last, he was going to receive the help he needed.

THE good Queen Isabella ordered two ships for Columbus and said she would pay for them. But money came from the royal treasury, and Queen Isabella did not have to sell her jewels.

The two ships cost about $14,000 in our money today. They were the finest of any ships sailing the sea in those days. They were about seventy to eighty feet long, and well equipped.

One ship was called *Santa Clara*. A man named **50** Niño (nee'-nyo) owned it, so everyone called it

Niña (nee′nya) for a nickname. Many people did not know Santa Clara was its real name. The second ship was called *Pinta* because the first man who owned it was named Pinto.

Columbus hired a third ship, the *Santa Maria.* We would call it the "Saint Mary." He bought this ship with money which he borrowed from his friends. Luis Santangel was one of the friends who helped him. The others were three brothers named Pinzon (peen-thone′).

At last Columbus was ready for his journey. The Queen gave him a letter to deliver to the Emeror of China. She promised Columbus one-tenth of all the gold discovered in the islands of the Indies. He asked to be made viceroy of the lands he should discover. He also asked to be called "Admiral of the Ocean Sea."

A Christian Departure. Early in the morning on August 3, 1492, Columbus attended Holy Mass and received Holy Communion. He placed his trust in God and set out with his crew from the harbor of Palos in Spain.

Three Ships upon the Ocean Blue. When the fleet reached the Canary Islands, the *Pinta* had a slight accident to her rudder. This was soon repaired. On September 9, Columbus' three ships left the Canary Islands and again faced the Sea of Darkness, as the Atlantic Ocean was called.

The little fleet was on unknown waters. Day after day, week after week, the ships sailed on.

September turned to October. Still only the wide, open sea lay before them. The ocean was smooth, the winds were fair, and the sky peaceful.

Early in October, the sailors began to complain. "Let us return to Spain," they said to Columbus. "We can see no land." The sailors were afraid they would be eaten by the sea-animals they had heard about. They thought they were lost and would never get home. But Columbus was not afraid. He placed his trust in God, and told the sailors: "Sail on! Sail on!"

Signs of Land. Now and then seaweed was seen floating on the water. Seaweed is usually a sign of land nearby. Yet no land was in sight. The men were discouraged and weary, but still their captain urged them to go on.

Then one day they saw a great number of birds flying westward. Columbus thought they must be flying in the direction of land. He gave orders to sail in the same direction.

At ten o'clock on the evening of October 11, 1492, Columbus was on deck. He thought he saw a light in the distance. Other sailors looked, but they could see nothing, for the light had disappeared. Columbus was hopeful.

Land Ho! Early in the morning of October 12, 1492, the lookout on the *Pinta* saw a sandy island in the distance. "Land, land!" came the cry from the ships. Everyone rushed on deck, eager and anxious to see land again.

Columbus' Faith Was Rewarded. Each night on the thirty-three-day voyage the sailors had joined Columbus in prayer. Each night the sailors lifted their voices in praise of the Blessed Mother. "Hail, Holy Queen" was the hymn they sang. We say that prayer at the end of Holy Mass. Mary did not fail Columbus and the sailors. She had guided them safely to land.

When daybreak came, Columbus, dressed in his rich velvet robes, stepped into a small boat and was rowed to shore. Immediately he knelt down and gave thanks to God. His crew kissed the ground, because they were so glad to be on land once again.

Every tree and plant was strange to him. Columbus realized that this land was an island. Columbus called it San Salvador, which means "Holy Saviour." He raised his sword and claimed the land for Spain.

He also planted a great cross in the soil of the land. The cross, you know, is the sign of our holy faith, the sign of Christians.

By raising this cross Columbus showed that he wanted to dedicate this land to Our Lord as well as claim it for Spain.

The natives of the island watched the crew kiss the ground. They watched Columbus plant the cross. These people were very shy, and seemed to be simple, gentle and peaceful.

Columbus wanted to make friends with them. **53**

He gave them some little red caps and glass beads for presents. They hung the beads around their necks as if they were most precious jewels. It was right for Columbus to be kind to these natives because all races belong to the same human family.

Columbus also hoped that some day these people would be Catholics.

Columbus thought he had reached India. That is why he called the natives Indians. They remained friendly to Columbus and his men. The Indians gave them parrots, cotton thread, darts, and many other things. They called the Spaniards "men from heaven."

Is This the Indies? Columbus knew that this land was not China. It was not the place described by Marco Polo in his famous book. Columbus thought he had discovered an island north of Japan, and therefore part of the East. If he sailed southwest, he thought he would come to Japan. If he missed Japan, he thought he would certainly land in China.

Columbus wrote in his journal, "I intend to go and see if I can find the Island of Japan." Do you know what a journal is? Why should Columbus keep one?

An Undelivered Letter. On October 14, Columbus left San Salvador. He sailed southwest. About fifteen miles from San Salvador he landed on an island which today we call Cuba. Columbus thought he had arrived in China. He sent messengers to deliver his letter to the Emperor. But no matter how far they traveled, they could not find the Emperor. The letter was never delivered.

During his travels Columbus saw the natives of Cuba smoking the dried leaves of the tobacco plant. This was the first time Columbus had seen anyone smoking, and it seemed to him quite a strange thing to do.

During this trip he also discovered the island of Haiti. He called this land Española (es-pan-yoe'-lah).

The Fate of the *Santa Maria*. On the night before Christmas, the *Santa Maria* was dashed to pieces 55 by the waves. All those on board were saved, but the ship was completely wrecked.

With the timbers left from the *Santa Maria*, Columbus built a fort at Española. He called the fort La Navidad (nah′-ve-dahd), which means "the Nativity," or "The Birth." It is the way to say Christmas in Spanish. He left some of the men to guard the fort. Columbus returned to Spain with the *Niña* and the *Pinta*.

A Joyful Return. Both ships anchored in the harbor of Palos in March, 1493. From Palos, Columbus and his men went to Barcelona, where he led a great procession, mounted on a white horse, wearing his rich velvet clothes. Truly he had earned the title "Admiral of the Ocean Sea."

Queen Isabella and King Ferdinand gave Columbus a royal welcome. Columbus bowed before the King and Queen. Then he showed them the things he brought back with him. These were six Indians, some parrots, strange plants and trees, and a little gold. Which of these was the most important? Why?

The whole Court listened to Columbus tell the story of the great voyage. The celebration closed with a prayer of praise and thanksgiving to God.

CHRISTIANITY FOR THE INDIANS

AFTER six months in Spain, Columbus set out again for the New World. This time many people were eager to go with him. They hoped they would find gold in the islands of the Indies. A fleet of seventeen vessels started for the new lands.

Holy Mass in a New Land. The six Indians were returning to their native land. They had been baptized and were now Christians.

Twelve mssionary priests went with the fleet. These priests hoped to teach religion to the Indians of the New World.

The ships landed at Puerto Rico. Father Buiul (boo′-ee-ool), who was the head of the missionaries, offered Holy Mass. This was the first Mass in the New World. Father Buiul was a Benedictine monk. A Benedictine is one who serves God by following the Rule of Saint Benedict.

From Puerto Rico, Columbus went to Española. He looked for the men he had left there, but did not find them. They had been killed in a quarrel with unfriendly Indians.

On the northern coast of the island he built a trading station, which he named Isabella. He also founded the town of San Domingo (doe-min′-go). Then he explored more of the surrounding country and discovered Jamaica. He spent three years in the New World at this time.

Chains for a Great Man. Columbus made two more voyages to America. On his third voyage, in 1498, he discovered the island of Trinidad. You can probably guess that he named it to honor the Holy Trinity. Then he sailed as far south as the continent of South America.

He returned to Haiti and found that some of the people were jealous of him, and told false stories about him. Others were disappointed because he did not discover gold and silver. His enemies put him in chains and sent him back to Spain.

Queen Isabella was greatly displeased to see Columbus in chains and released him.

In May, 1502, Columbus set out on his last voyage. He sailed along the eastern coast of Central America. He did not find China, as he thought he would.

Columbus returned to Spain and died, poor and forsaken by all. Everyone was disappointed that

Columbus had not discovered gold. Up to the time of his death, Columbus thought he had reached some islands in the Indies.

A Name by Mistake. Shortly after this, a man named Americus Vespucius (ves-pew'-shus) explored the coast of South America. When he returned to Europe he wrote a letter to a friend. In this letter he described the lands he had explored. He said the new land looked like a great continent.

A German map maker read the letter. He thought that Americus Vespucius had discovered the land he described. The map maker thought this land should be named after Americus Vespucius. So in his new maps, he gave the name "America" to the land that Columbus had really discovered.

Then the map maker found out his mistake. But his maps had been distributed all over Europe! It was too late. The land of Columbus would always be called "America," the name which it received by mistake. Sometimes today people call our country Columbia. Can you tell the reason why?

AMERICA THE BEAUTIFUL

COLUMBUS did not find the gold he sought, but found instead a land which was greater than gold.

If Columbus could visit our land today he would hardly believe that this was the land he discovered. Airplanes, skyscrapers, and television would be greater marvels to Columbus than they are even to us.

Yet these things alone do not make our land greater than gold, because they can be bought with money. We live in a land of freedom. Freedom cannot be bought in a store like a wrist-watch or a diamond ring. It is freedom that makes our land greater than gold. God has given every man certain rights which no one can take away from him. We have the right to live as we know we ought to live. We can own property, such as our homes, our television sets, our automobiles. We can speak, think, and act as God tells us we ought to act. As Catholics, we can seek happiness in being faithful to our holy religion. We must thank God that we can enjoy these rights, which no gold or riches can buy.

Our Land and Our Lady. You know that this series of histories is called "Land of Our Lady Series."

It has been called by this title because Our Blessed Mother is the Patroness of the United States.

Under her title of Our Lady of the Immaculate Conception, she is asked to watch over this country and protect it.

From very early times, Our Lady has been thought of and prayed to. You remember how Co-

lumbus and his sailors sang her hymn, the "Hail,

Holy Queen," each night at dusk. They were asking Our Lady to take care of them on the dark and unknown seas.

You will read later on, in this book, how other explorers named places after her. For example, the first name given to the Mississippi River was that of the Immaculate Conception.

Many other places have been named after her, but when people came here who did not love her, they changed these names.

It is a good thing for Catholic boys and girls always to remember that this is Our Lady's land. We should pray to her and ask her to make this land strong and holy.

Land of Liberty. This land which Columbus discovered is a land of liberty. During the years after our land was discovered many people came here from all parts of the world.

Some of these people came to build homes and raise families. Others came to make money and seek riches and fame. Some were even debtors from English prisons.

One of the other main reasons why people came here was to find freedom to worship God.

Improving Your Vocabulary

accompanied	approve	journal
saddlebags	Moors	wharf
monastery	San Salvador	counsellors
map maker	Española	wreckage
conqueror	hemisphere	viceroy

Use Your Thinking Cap

1. Columbus was born in Italy. How did he happen to sail from Spain?
2. Why did Columbus think he would reach the Indies by sailing west?
3. Name some places named in honor of Columbus. If you need help, look it up in your geography.
4. Why was the land Columbus discovered more important than finding a route to the East?
5. Find in your geography the explanation of how the Indians first came to America.

Something to Do

Explain to the class how to use a compass.

Write a diary of Marco Polo's journey to Cathay.

Pretend that you were with Columbus on his first voyage. Write a letter to your parents in Spain, telling them about the landing on San Salvador.

On an outline map of the Eastern Hemisphere, paste pictures of the goods found by merchants in the different countries of the Orient. Collect pictures of ships used in the days of Columbus.

High Lights of the Unit

Turn to the outline on page 11 of this unit. The important parts of the unit are found on that page. After you have studied the important facts listed in the outline, write the story of this unit in three paragraphs.

UNIT ONE—MASTERY TEST

GOD'S GIFT—AMERICA

I. Number the lines on a sheet of paper 1 to 20. After each number, write the answer to that question.

1. What are people called who make journeys to holy places?

2. Why did the Christians of Europe call Palestine "The Holy Land"?

3. Who were the Christian people in Europe who fought in Palestine?

4. By what other name was the East called?

5. Which nation was attacking the holy places in Palestine?

6. Who was the discoverer of an all-water route to India?

7. Which invention helped the sailors to know direction?

8. What is the name of the book written by Marco Polo?

9. Who discovered a cape on the southern tip of Africa?

10. To which eastern country did Marco Polo travel?

11. Who were the first Christians to visit North America?

12. What Portuguese prince trained other sailors?

13. Was America or India discovered first?

14. Who lived in America before Europeans came here?

15. What does San Salvador mean?

16. In what country was Columbus born?

17. Who was the Franciscan priest who spoke to the Queen for Columbus?

18. How many voyages did Columbus make to the New World?

19. What was the name of the first fort Columbus established?

20. Which cities in Italy were rivals in trade?

II. Write the numbers 1 to 10 in a column. After each number, write the correct letter that answers each item.

1. An astrolabe shows
   a. right direction
   b. stars at night
   c. position of the sun or stars
   d. distance from land

2. The equator is
   a. an invention for sailors
   b. a place on the Atlantic Ocean
   c. a line on the globe from north to south
   d. an imaginary circle drawn around the center of the globe

3. A caravan is
   a. a group of Crusaders trading with merchants
   b. a group of travelers
   c. cargo on ships
   d. a product of Palestine

4. A merchant is one who
   a. always sails the high seas
   b. tells people the best places for trade
   c. buys and sells articles
   d. studies maps and charts of trade routes

5. Christianity means
   a. Christians
   b. the religion of Christians
   c. followers of Christ
   d. the land where Christ lived

6. A monastery is
   a. the home of Columbus
   b. the home of Queen Isabella
   c. the place where monks live
   d. the palace of Prince Henry

7. A trade route is a road traveled by
    a. Turks in the Holy Land
    b. Italians in Europe
    c. Prince Henry in Africa
    d. merchants

8. A Crusader is one who
    a. traded with the East
    b. tried to save the Holy Places
    c. fought the Mohammedans in Africa
    d. sailed with the Northmen

9. A watchword is
    a. a motto for a group of people
    b. the title of a book
    c. a signal to begin a battle
    d. a sign of danger

10. A viceroy is
    a. an instrument
    b. a leader at Court
    c. a governor of a province
    d. the emperor of a great country

III. On separate lines, write the numbers 1 to 8. Write the correct letter that answers each item.

1. Which of these events occurred first?
    a. the fall of Constantinople
    b. the beginning of exploration in America
    c. the first settlement in America
    d. Columbus' first meeting with the Indians

2. Columbus landed on
    a. a peninsula
    b. the continent of South America
    c. an island of the East Indies
    d. Española

3. The name America was given to our land because
    a. Columbus wanted it called by that name
    b. Americus Vespucius discovered the land   **65**

    c. a map maker thought Americus Vespu-
      cius discovered our land

    d. Americus Vespucius was the first Euro-
      pean to land on the mainland

4. Land of the Indies means
    a. India, China, and Palestine
    b. China, Persia, and Russia
    c. India, Constantinople, and Palestine
    d. India, Japan, and China

5. Crusaders fought in Palestine because
    a. it was not so far as China
    b. the Turks would not fight on their own
      land
    c. they wanted to rescue the Holy Places
    d. they wanted to own the country of Pal-
      estine

6. An important result of the Crusades was
    a. the Holy Places were rescued
    b. many Turks were converted
    c. the Crusaders became friendly with the
      Turks
    d. people of Europe saw riches they never
      saw before

7. The fall of Constantinople was a misfortune
for Europeans because
    a. they were afraid the Turks would also
      destroy Italy
    b. that city had so many beautiful churches
    c. there was no other city in Asia Minor
    d. land routes to the Orient were closed

8. Columbus did not reach the East by sailing
west because
    a. he was shipwrecked
    b. his sailors made him turn back

    c. he had sailed in the wrong direction

    d. a great body of land lay between the East and the West

IV. Answer the following questions. Use complete sentences.

    a. Why did most of the people of Europe first read Marco Polo's book many years after it was written?

    b. Why did Italy lose trade with the East?

    c. Which of Columbus' four voyages to America was the most important? Why?

    d. Why were the compass and the astrolabe useful inventions to Columbus?

    e. How did God bring good out of the European desire for riches?

V. Match the following. After each number write the numbers 1 to 5 in a column. Place the name of the continent which answers each item correctly. A continent may be used more than once.

Location	*Name of Continent*
1. South of Europe	**a.** North America
2. East of Europe	**b.** Asia
3. North of Africa	**c.** Europe
4. Where the Holy Land is	**d.** Africa
5. Where Columbus found Indians	

Do the same with the following countries.

Location	*Country*
6. Bordered on west by Atlantic Ocean	**e.** Spain
	f. India
7. Southwest of China	**g.** Portugal
8. South of Germany	**h.** Italy
9. West of Spain	
10. North of Indian Ocean	

Our Lady
of
Fatima

Pray for us

PRAYER

IMMACULATE Virgin, refuge of sinners, thou who, in order to atone for the injuries done to Almighty God and the evils inflicted on men by sin, didst accept with resignation the death of thy divine Son, be ever propitious towards us, and in heaven, where thou dost reign gloriously, continue in our behalf thy work of zeal and love. We would be thy children: do thou still show thyself a Mother. Obtain from Jesus, our divine Redeemer, that He may be pleased to apply to our souls the fruits of His passion and death, and deliver us from the bonds of our iniquities. May He be our light in midst of darkness, our strength in weakness, our refuge in the midst of peril; may He strengthen us by His grace and love in this world, and grant us to love Him, see Him and possess Him in the world to come. Amen. *(500 days)*

UNIT TWO

WITH SADDLES AND SANDALS

CHAPTER I — AN INDIAN TALE COMES TRUE
Balboa discovered the Pacific Ocean by crossing the Isthmus of Panama.

CHAPTER II — EXPLORERS ON LAND AND SEA
Magellan proved the world was round by sailing around it.
Cortes conquered Mexico in 1521.
Cortes built Mexico City.

CHAPTER III — PATHWAYS IN THE SOUTHEAST
Ponce de Leon discovered Florida.
De Soto explored the southeastern part of our country.
De Soto discovered the Mississippi River.
Some of De Soto's men returned to Mexico.
Father Cancer was martyred in Florida in 1549.
In 1565, the oldest colony in what is now the United States was established at St. Augustine.

Florida became the property of England in
1763, but later was returned to Spain.

CHAPTER IV—PIONEER TRAILS OF THE SOUTHWEST

Coronado explored the Southwest, and discovered the Grand Canyon of the Colorado.

Father John of Padilla was the first martyr on the land of the United States.

The second Spanish colony in the United
States was founded at Santa Fe.

Jesuits and Franciscans labored in Arizona
for the Indians.

Father Antonio Margil and other Franciscans labored for many years among the
Indians in Texas.

By 1853, the great Southwest had become
the property of the United States.

CHAPTER V —WHERE THE MISSION BELLS RING

Father Junipero Serra established his first
mission at San Diego in 1769.

Twenty-one missions for the Indians were
built along the King's Highway.

California became a province of Mexico in
1821.

The United States acquired California in
1848.

UNIT TWO

Tales of Trials and Triumph. After Columbus discovered the New World, Spaniards came over and settled in Cuba, Haiti, and Jamaica. Later the Spaniards explored the mainland of the continent. They found gold and silver in its soil. They had many adventures in Mexico and Peru.

We owe much to the Spaniards, because they also traveled throughout the southern part of our own country. Everywhere they went they tried to spread the Kingdom of God upon earth.

Everywhere the soldiers went, missionary priests went with them. Many missionary priests and Brothers worked among the Indians from Florida to California. Many were martyred in this great land.

Lands to the north of Mexico were also explored. Missionaries came with the explorers. One of these missionaries gave his life for the Faith among the Indians of Kansas. He is the first martyr in the United States.

Missionaries from Mexico went to Texas to teach and baptize the Indians there. In the early

71

days of Santa Fé, Franciscans served the natives of New Mexico. In Arizona, Father Kino, the "horseback Padre," preached the Gospel of Christ to the Indians.

The word of God was preached in all the lands explored by Spaniards. Before the great United States became a nation, Indians in California heard the call of Father Serra's mission bells and came to the feet of Christ. Father Serra built many missions. He called the road from one mission another the King's Highway. By this name he gave special honor to Christ the King.

In this unit you will read of the trials and triumphs of those who came to America with saddles and sandals.

The reason we speak of "saddles" and "sandals" in this unit is because many of the explorers traveled on horseback through our country.

The "saddles" therefore represent the explorers.

The sandals refer to the open shoes worn by the early missionaries, especially the Franciscans. Sandals are still a part of the dress of the Franciscan Friars.

Thus, the "sandals" represent the priests, whether they were Franciscans or belonged to other orders.

The missionaries came to spread the kingdom of God. They were glad to work for no other reward but that.

CHAPTER I

AN INDIAN TALE COMES TRUE

More Discoveries. In the first unit, we learned about the discovery of a new world. Columbus thought he had reached the Indies. He had really discovered America.

Columbus' discovery was a wonderful event, but there were still more discoveries ahead. They began with the story an Indian chief told to a group of Spaniards. He told of a great ocean and of a land where there was much gold. Because the Spaniards believed this story, they discovered an ocean and a fortune for the King of Spain!

What a surprise it must have been to learn that a great ocean lay beyond the land discovered by Columbus! The Spaniards began to learn that this new land was not really the Indies.

The Spaniards sailed south on this new ocean. They found the land of gold told about by the Indian. More gold was obtained from this land of Peru than they could ever secure from the East.

In this chapter you will learn more about the tale of the Indian, and what happened because the Spaniards believed this story.

AFTER the death of Columbus, people from Europe came to live on the islands he had discovered in the Caribbean Sea. They were called the "Mother Isles" because the first Spanish settlers lived there. From these islands a knowledge of the true religion was spread to the neighboring islands.

The Man in the Barrel. About 1510, a group of Spaniards left Española to make a settlement. They were well out from port when the top of one barrel stored on deck began to open. Off came the lid, and a man climbed out of the barrel. You can imagine how surprised everybody was.

The captain asked the man who he was and why he hid in the barrel. The man replied that he was Vasco de Balboa from the island of Española.

He said he had heard about the new trip and decided to go with these men to other lands. However, he could not leave the country until he paid many debts which he owed. So he hid in an empty barrel until the ship was well out from port. In this way he hoped to escape unnoticed.

The captain was angry with Balboa and said he would put him off the ship at the first deserted island. Balboa begged for mercy. Finally the captain allowed him to continue the journey.

The First Settlement on Panama. Just as the ship was in sight of land, there arose a great storm, which completely destroyed the vessel. When the

74

sailors reached shore, the captain would not let the Spaniards trade for gold with the Indians. This displeased the Spaniards very much. They sent their captain to another port and chose Balboa for their leader.

These Spaniards made a settlement at Darien. They called their settlement Santa Maria. This was the first settlement made on land that was not an island. On your map you will see that Darien is on the mainland of the continent.

A GREAT OCEAN

The Indian Tale. One day some of Balboa's men were quarreling over a piece of gold they had discovered. An Indian chief came along. He said to them, "You will find plenty of gold in a land to the south. First, you must march to the west over the mountains. Then you will come to a great ocean. Then march south for six suns. Powerful kings rule the land and you will need a large army to conquer them."

Balboa believed this tale of the Indian. He decided to find the great sea on the other side of the mountains. He also decided to try to find the rich land of gold.

Crossing the Mountains. One morning in 1513, Balboa and his men put on their heavy, shining steel armor. First they had to go through a deep forest. Then they trudged through swamps. Onward they went. Soon they came to the mountains. **75**

Up and up they climbed. Each step was more difficult thon the one before.

Soon they were near the top of the highest peak. Balboa wanted to be the first European to see this new ocean, so he went ahead. This was the man who once hid in a barrel. Soon he was to discover a great ocean.

The Work of God's Hands. Balboa saw the blue ocean stretched in the warm sunlight. It was, indeed, a great ocean, something only God could create. Then Balboa called his men. Together they knelt and thanked God for this great discovery.

It took them two days to reach the waters below. When they came to the shore, Balboa raised a cross. Then he waded into the water. He waved his sword over it and claimed the sea for the King of Spain. He called it the South Sea because it extended to the south.

Balboa's men were happy over their new discovery. They thought this ocean might lead to China or India. Balboa knew he had found a short land route that led him from one ocean to another. Even in those early days Balboa said a canal ought to be built across this narrow neck of land. No canal was built there until hundreds of years later.

77

In 1519, the city of Panama was built at the place where Balboa waded into the South Sea. It was the first city built on the shores of the new ocean.

Death of Balboa. After Balboa discovered the South Sea, he planned to sail this sea until he came to the Land of Gold.

When Balboa returned to Darien to obtain men and supplies for his journey, he learned that a new governor had been appointed. The governor was not kind to Balboa because he believed untrue stories about him. In 1519, Balboa was arrested, given an unfair trial, and put to death.

PIZARRO, A NOBLEMAN

Sailing South on the Pacific. A man named Pizarro was with Balboa when he discovered the great new ocean. He knew about Balboa's plans to find the Land of Gold to the south, so he decided to find that gold.

The governor of Darien gave Pizarro one ship and a crew for his voyage. There was not half enough food for the long trip, and, before long, Pizarro was forced to return. Pizarro started for the Land of Gold a second time. Again, his crew became hungry and discontented. The governor heard about this, and commanded Pizarro to return.

The crew were ashore when they received the message from the governor. At once, they prepared to board the ship and sail for home. But

Pizarro had no intention of returning. However, he needed men.

Crossing the Line. Pizarro had a plan. He called the men together. He drew a line on the ground. Then he said to his men: "All men who are brave, cross this line and follow me. I do not promise you an easy time. There will be plenty of hard work and danger. Maybe we shall almost starve before we reach the Land of Gold! Only those who are brave will cross this line."

Less than twenty men walked across the line. About one hundred seventy men returned to the ship and sailed away. Still Pizarro did not give up. He and his followers stayed on the island.

On to the Land of Gold. Four long, dreary months passed. Then a ship came to take them all back home. But Pizarro was determined not to give up his search for gold. He and his men boarded the ship. Instead of sailing for home, they sailed farther and farther south. At last they came to a country with green fields. Pizarro sent two soldiers ahead to see if there was any gold on this land. They returned with tales of great riches.

Pizarro wanted the riches of this country. He knew he could not conquer the Indians with just a few men. He returned home and told the governor about the Land of Gold. He asked the governor for more help, but the governor refused.

Help from Spain. Pizarro sailed to Spain. He asked the King for help to conquer the Land of

Gold. When the King heard his story, he gave him the money and soldiers he needed. The King also made Pizarro a nobleman of Spain.

Pizarro returned to Panama. Then he set out to conquer the Indians in the land of Gold. This time he was well prepared.

PIZARRO IN PERU

Inca and the Incas. The Land of Gold was the country which we call Peru. The Indians who lived there were called Incas. Their chief was called the Inca. The Incas did not know the great value of all the gold and silver they possessed. They used it only for ornaments and decorations. The Spaniards thought this a very foolish way to use gold.

The Inca lived in a palace decorated with gold. This palace was called the Temple of the Sun.

When Pizarro landed in Peru, he and his men saddled their horses and started for the place where the Inca was living. They met many Indians on the way. These Indians had never seen horses or guns before and were greatly frightened. When the Incas saw Pizarro, they thought he was the son of the Sky-God, and that his horses were monsters.

When Pizarro came near the Inca's home, he made a camp. Then he invited the Inca chief to dinner. During the meal, he made the Inca his prisoner. He thought he could capture the Indians' gold more easily if they were left without a leader. The Inca was placed in a large room. The Incas soon became helpless without a leader.

Pizarro's Promise. When the Inca chief learned that Pizarro wanted gold, he said to Pizarro, "If you free me, I will fill this room with gold for you." Placing his hand up high on the wall, the chief

added, "I will fill it up to this mark. The next room I will fill with silver." Pizarro said he would free the Inca if he kept his promise.

Then the Indians worked hard. They walked for miles and miles carrying heavy loads of gold. They brought it to the Spaniards' storehouses. The Spaniards never dreamed that so much gold existed anywhere.

Now it was time for Pizarro to keep the promise he had made to the Inca. His conscience should have told him that the law of God bound him to keep his promise. But Pizarro was greedy. Instead of freeing the Inca, Pizarro killed him! He said he was afraid the Inca would gather his Indians together and attack the small army of the Spaniards.

The Indians were very angry when they heard of their chief's death. They destroyed the Spaniards' storehouses in revenge for the death of their chief.

Fall of the Inca Empire. Since the Incas had no leader, it was easy for Pizarro to conquer them. This happened in 1539. Pizarro took all the gold mines of Peru.

Now Pizarro showed more cruelty and unkindness. He had the Indians work in the mines as slaves. He made them melt the gold and silver that came from the mines. They made it into bricks and bars. Then all this gold was taken by the Indians to the city of Panama. At Panama it was loaded into large Spanish ships called galleons. The galleons then carried the gold to Spain.

Later, Pizarro built the city of Lima, near the coast. This city became the capital of Peru.

Death of Pizarro. Some of Pizarro's people did not trust him, and others were jealous of him. One

day, a group of his enemies surrounded him and

killed him. He died as he was making the sign of the cross in his own blood.

The Riches of Peru. For almost two hundred years after Pizarro's death, Spain got gold and silver from Peru. This gold made Spain a very wealthy nation.

But the greatest riches of Peru did not come from gold and silver. Peru's greatest riches came from the Catholic faith. Our holy religion was brought to the people of Peru by the missionaries who came there with explorers.

Some of these explorers were greedy and cruel, like Pizarro. But missionary priests always went with the expeditions. These priests did all they could to make the explorers be kind to the Indians. These missionaries also taught the Indians about Our Lord and His Church.

Long after Pizarro died, the Catholic faith still lived on in Peru. When Spain owned the land, more and more priests came to convert the Indians. Priests also opened a University in the city of Lima in 1551. By 1700 it had over two thousand students.

Many holy people lived in Peru. Among them was Saint Rose of Lima. Saint Rose was the first person born in the New World to become a canonized saint.

Another holy person from Peru was Blessed Martin de Porres (day pore'-res). He spent his life helping the poor.

These are the real riches of Peru. They are more valuable than all the gold Pizarro found.

The lives of these good and holy people show us that riches are only valuable if they help us to live better lives and do good for others.

Some of the explorers were so greedy that they forgot about this. They were looking only for gold and riches. Then they became cruel to the Indians they found in the New World.

The Church, however, did all she could to make these explorers be kind to the Indians. That is why missionaries accompanied all voyages of exploration.

The explorers often forgot that all men are the children of God. By being cruel to the Indians, they were committing many wrongs. Some of these men were punished even in this life. They were hated by their followers, and some of them were even murdered. You can see, therefore, that it is unwise to be cruel and greedy since this offends God and is punished by Him.

Word Study

imprison	misfortune	galleons
instructed	revenge	enemies
mainland	Inca	canonized

Talking Over the Lesson

1. Which discovery do you think was greater, that of Balboa or Pizarro?
2. What lesson do we learn from the Indian's tale to Balboa?
3. What did Pizarro do when the governor of Panama refused to help him?
4. What did Pizarro do to challenge his men to stay with him on the island?
5. How did Pizarro get gold from the Incas?
6. What were the real riches of Peru?

Studying the Lesson

1. On the map, find the place where Balboa landed. Why was this an important settlement?
2. Find the path of Balboa in search for the great ocean.
3. Find Peru on the map of South America. Find the capital of Peru.
4. Make a time-line. On it place the dates on which Balboa discovered the Pacific Ocean and Pizarro discovered Peru. As you move along in this unit, there will be more dates to add to your time-line of Spanish explorers and colonizers.

CHAPTER II

EXPLORERS ON LAND AND SEA

Looking Over the Chapter. Great riches came to Spain because two of her explorers decided to find out if an Indian tale were true.

Other explorers set out to find fame and fortune for themselves and Spain. A great captain sailed the new ocean and completed the first journey around the world. Another set out to explore the land north of Panama and found more gold and silver for Spain.

In this chapter you will learn how Magellan (ma-jel'-an) proved to the people of Europe that the world is round. He proved that America is really a new world. You will also read about an explorer named Cortes (core-tes') who conquered Mexico for Spain.

MAGELLAN'S PLAN

The Sailor Boy. In the first unit you learned how Da Gama brought riches to Portugal. Among those who heard of his journey, was a young Portuguese sailor named Magellan.

Before long, this young sailor had a ship of his

own. He became one of the best captains on the sea. He used Da Gama's route to India. He sailed even farther than Da Gama. He brought greater riches to Portugal than any other sailor before him had ever done.

When Magellan returned to Portugal from India, he was told how Balboa discovered a new ocean. The first thing Magellan did was to mark on his map the place of the new sea. Then he studied his maps harder than ever.

Magellan had a plan. He would first find a water route around the land of Columbus. He would then sail on the new ocean until he reached the East. From the Indies he would return home by the route he knew so well around the Cape of Good Hope.

Looking for Help. In great haste and excitement Magellan went to the King of Portugal. He asked for help, but the King refused. The King of Portugal was satisfied with the route discovered by Da Gama.

Magellan went to Spain. King Charles listened to him. He gave Magellan five ships with crews and plenty of supplies. The King told Magellan to find a southwest passage to India.

DISCOVERING A NEW STRAIT

In 1519, Magellan sailed from Spain. About three hundred men were with him on the ships. Magellan took the course of Columbus across the

Atlantic Ocean. Then he turned south and went along the eastern coast of South America. As the ships sailed down the coast, everyone watched for a water passage to the sea of Balboa. They looked and looked, but could find none.

At one spot along the coast they saw on the shore some very large men. Magellan landed and spoke to them by means of signs. Their feet were so large that the crew called them "Big Feet." Today we call that land Patagonia, but Magellan called it "the land of the big feet."

For many, many weeks, Magellan and his men sailed on. Yet there was no sign of the waterway they were trying to find.

A Hard Winter. In December they reached a bay in the southern part of South America. Here Magellan stopped and anchored for the winter. Here one of his ships turned back. The rest of Magellan's men also wanted to go home, but Magellan refused.

In the spring they started sailing south again. They still hoped to find a waterway through the land to the other ocean.

The Connecting Strait. At last they came to a narrow channel of water. They did not know whether or not it reached Balboa's sea. They entered this crooked waterway with its steep, rocky banks. One ship, the *San Antonio,* turned back when they reached this dangerous spot.

As Magellan and his crew sailed on, they saw

Indian campfires on the shore. On they went, through the passage, until they came to the great sea! This narrow waterway on which they sailed connects the Atlantic and Pacific Oceans. Since that time it has been called the Strait of Magellan. It took Magellan thirty-eight days to sail through. It was October, 1520.

The crew thought that the island to the south was a big continent. This place is called Tierra del Fuego. It means Land of Fires. Can you find Tierra del Fuego on your map?

Magellan now saw for the first time the ocean Balboa had discovered. He called it the Pacific Ocean, because it looked so peaceful.

Again the sailors wanted to return home. They were satisfied that they had found a way to the other ocean. Magellan said, "We shall continue our journey even if we have to eat the leather from the fastenings on the ship."

One ship turned back that night. Now there were only three ships to brave the dangers of the great voyage.

PROOF OF A ROUND WORLD

THE food supply was now very low. The ships sailed for weeks along the western coast of South America. Finally, Magellan's words came true. The sailors were so hungry, they had to chew pieces of leather cut from the rigging. They dragged pieces of leather in the ocean until they became soft. Then they were dried, cooked, and eaten.

About fourteen months had passed since Magellan and his men had left South America. They wondered if they would ever see land again. Then one day the lookouts spied some islands in the distance.

Better Than Gold. The land spotted by Magellan's men was the group of islands we call the Marianas. If your father or big brother fought in the Pacific during World War II, he may be able to tell you much about these islands. He may also be able to tell you about the work our Catholic missionaries are doing in these lands.

90 Magellan's men obtained food from these

islands. For the first time in their lives they saw bananas. They also filled their ships with cocoanuts, milk, figs, rice, fish, and fresh water. They were so hungry that the food was much more valuable to them than the gold they were seeking. When you are hungry would you rather have some food or a piece of gold?

The Work of Thieves. While Magellan and his men were on the islands, hundreds of brown men crept aboard their ships and stole everything they could get their hands on. Because of this, Magellan called the islands "Islands of Thieves." The name still remains. They are known as the Ladrones (la-droe'-nes), the Spanish word for thieves.

More Islands Discovered. A little later, in 1521, Magellan discovered more islands. These were the Philippine Islands. Magellan was now very close to the Spice Islands but, of course, he did not know that he was.

The natives of the Philippine Islands were friendly. They came to meet Magellan and his men. They had strange boats, with sails made of palm-leaves.

Magellan gave the natives red caps, mirrors, combs, and bells. The natives gave him fish, bananas, cocoanuts, and a jar of wine made from palm juice.

Magellan and his men made friends with these natives. A priest who was with Magellan's expedi-   **91** tion baptized the native chief of this friendly tribe. Many of the other people in the tribe also became baptized Catholics.

Death of Magellan. While Magellan was in the Philippine Islands, war broke out between Magellan's native friends and another tribe. Magellan fought on the side of the friendly Indians and was killed in one of the battles. The Spaniards then chose a new leader.

To make matters worse, one of the ships began to leak so badly, it could not be repaired. The Spaniards burnt this ship. Now only two ships were left to continue the journey.

On to the East Indies! Soon the ships reached the Spice Islands. Here the sailors obtained many precious articles and products. Here one of the ships was captured by enemies. Only one ship was left. The men loaded this ship with spices and then decided to head for home.

The next stop was India. They remained there only a short time. They wanted to return to Spain after their great journey around the world.

They had crossed the Pacific Ocean, which is twice as wide as the great Atlantic. They had reached the East by sailing west. They were the first to sail around the world! The voyage proved that America was a New World. This was indeed a great discovery.

The ship with its thirty-one men landed in

Spain on September 8, 1522. These men had been

away from home for three years. The crew went to the shrine of Our Lady of Victory and thanked God for their safe return.

SEARCHING FOR GOLD IN THE NEW LAND

A Lover of Adventure. Hernando Cortes (ehr-nan'-doe core-tes') was born in Spain. He was a very young boy at the time Columbus returned from his first voyage. Cortes loved adventure. He wanted to become a soldier and a great leader. He liked to ride fine horses. He liked to hunt and to play with guns and swords.

When he was nineteen years old he went to the West Indies. These islands had been discovered by Columbus. The governor of the West Indies had heard that Cortes was very brave.

The governor sent the young man to stop a rebellion among the Indians. Cortes soon put an end to the rebellion.

The Spaniards had heard that Mexico was a very rich land and had buildings of gold. The governor sent Cortes to conquer this land. He set out with eleven ships, six hundred Spaniards, some Indians, and sixteen horses. He also took with him dogs, cannon, and ammunition.

A Weary March. On Palm Sunday, 1519, Cortes landed on the shore of Mexico. His first act on landing was to burn his ships! He did this to be sure that his men could not turn back.

Then he said: "Gentlemen, let us follow our 93

banner which is the sign of the Holy Cross, for with it we shall conquer."

Many tribes of Indians lived in this land. The most powerful tribe was the Aztecs (az'-teks). The chief of this tribe was named Montezuma (mon-teh-zoo'-ma). He was very tall and handsome, but very cruel and crafty. The other Indian tribes were afraid of the Aztecs because they were so cruel.

Cortes had heard that Montezuma and the Aztecs were very rich, so he decided he would try to conquer them and take their gold.

Montezuma lived in a city far from the coast where Cortes landed. He left fifty men to guard the coast and then he and his army began to march across the country.

On the way, Cortes met many different tribes of Indians. He had battles with some of these tribes. During these battles the Spaniards rode horses and wore armor. They also used guns and cannon. The horses frightened these Indians as much as they had frightened the Incas in Peru. The Indians were terrified by the noise of the guns.

A Scene of Great Beauty. Each day, Cortes came nearer to the city where Montezuma lived. He passed through villages which were surrounded by great white walls. He saw beautiful temples and houses built of red or white stone.

Finally, beautiful Mexico City was in sight. It **94** was built on islands in the middle of a lake. Five paved bridges led to it. Along the streets and canals were great palaces built of red stone. One of these palaces was large enough to hold the entire army of Cortes.

There were towers, castles, and gardens everywhere. There were gardens on the roofs, on the walls, and even floating on the lake.

The temple rose high above the other buildings. Cortes and his men were surprised at the beauty of it all.

Montezuma lived in this beautiful city. He knew that Cortes and his men were powerful. He knew he would have to make friends with them, for he dared not fight against them. Montezuma went out to meet Cortes and gave him many fine presents. Later he gave Cortes a great feast in his honor.

Trouble Ahead. Cortes began to fear that the Aztecs would attack his army. So he decided to make Montezuma a prisoner. Cortes thought that the Indians would not fight without their leader. While he was at dinner, Cortes gave a signal, and the Spanish soldiers surrounded Montezuma and captured him.

In the meantime, the governor of the West Indies became very envious of Cortes. He sent another leader with twelve ships and nine hundred men to capture Cortes and conquer Mexico.

The new army landed at Vera Cruz (vay′ra crooth) and captured the men Cortes had left to guard the coast. In the darkness of the night, one of Cortes' men escaped, and went ahead to tell Cortes about the new leader.

Cortes thought quickly. With three hundred men he set out to meet his enemy. He left a few men in the city to guard the prisoner Montezuma.

Enlarging the Army. Cortes came upon the new leader's army at night. Cortes quickly defeated this army and imprisoned the leader at Vera Cruz. Then he took the Spanish soldiers into his army. Cortes then had a greater army than ever before.

A Surprise Battle. When Cortes returned to Mexico City, he found that some of his men had fought with the Aztecs and angered them. Then the Aztecs had attacked the Spaniards.

Stones, arrows, and spears rained down upon them from the roofs of houses, windows and towers. The Spaniards turned their guns and cannon on the Indians. Many of the Indians were killed.

Cortes and his men went to the building where Montezuma was a prisoner. Cortes sent Montezuma out on the wall to tell the Indians to stop fighting. The Aztec chief went to a high place and called for silence. He told the Indians he was only the guest of the Spaniards. He told the Indians to stop fighting.

But the Indians no longer treated Montezuma as their leader. They thought he had forsaken them.

Instead of obeying him, they threw stones at him. One of the stones hit him and killed him.

It looked as though all was over for Cortes. The Indians began to fight harder, and drove Cortes from the city. But he did not give up. He prepared for greater battles which were to come.

Final Victory. Finally, after three months of hard fighting, Cortes captured Mexico City. Later Cortes sent all the gold and silver mined in Mexico to Vera Cruz. There it was loaded on the Spanish galleons and taken to Spain.

Governor of Mexico. Cortes hurried to Spain and told King Charles about his victory. He also gave him a large quantity of gold.

The King made Cortes governor of New Spain,

as Mexico was then called. In those days Mexico included all of Mexico, Arizona, New Mexico and California.

Growth of Mexico. Mexico became a Spanish colony. Because of the great wealth in Mexico, it did not take long for people from Spain to come over and settle there. Cortes rebuilt Mexico City. He built a great cathedral where the Aztec temple had been. Mexico City grew up around this beautiful cathedral.

Missionaries came to Mexico and taught the Indians about Christianity. Soon many of these people became Catholics.

Our Lady Appears in Mexico. One day an Indian named Juan was hurrying to Mexico City to go to Mass. As he was going down a big hill outside the city, the Blessed Virgin appeared to him. She told him to go to the Bishop of Mexico City and tell him that she wanted a church built at this very spot. She called herself "Holy Mary of Guadalupe" (gwad-a-loo'-pay).

The Blessed Mother told Juan to gather roses and take them to the bishop. Now Juan knew that no roses were growing at that time of the year, but he started to look for some. Sure enough, there was a rosebush covered with beautiful roses.

He gathered the roses and put them in his big cloak. Then he carried them to the bishop. When he opened his cloak to show the roses to the bishop, another wonderful thing happened. Juan's cloak had a beautiful picture on it. It was a picture of Our Lady as she appeared to Juan.

A church was built in Our Lady's honor, and ever since people have gone there on pilgrimages. The Blessed Mother has performed many miracles for those who visit this shrine.

Our Lady showed that she wanted the people of the New World to be strong in their faith. She wanted us to know that the New World is indeed the Land of Our Lady.

End of Spanish Rule. Spain ruled Mexico until 1821. Then it became an independent country. The Spanish brought the Catholic religion and the Spanish language, laws, and customs to Mexico through the years. Spain has truly left our continent a great heritage.

Our Heritage. The first discoverers of our country were Catholics. Along with them came the missionaries, who converted the Indians and kept alive the faith among the early settlers.

Many of the missionaries became martyrs for the Catholic faith.

The faith was planted in America from the very beginning. As we have learned, many places were named after Our Lord, or Our Lady, or the saints.

Such names were given by the explorers because they wanted to honor Our Lord and His Mother.

We should always remember this, so that we

too can honor Our Lord and the Blessed Mother. This shows that America is truly a Land of Our Lady.

The Spanish did a great deal to help our Catholic faith to grow and develop in the New World. And then, to show that she loved America and its people, Our Lady appeared to Juan, the Mexican Indian at Guadalupe.

We should always remember these things. As Americans, we want our country to be good and holy and happy. The best way to help our country is by being good Catholics. Then we will be good Americans.

The best things a country can have are good citizens, who love God and worship Him. No matter how rich a country is, no matter how powerful it is, it is not a good country unless its citizens love and worship God.

All the riches in the world are worth nothing if they have been obtained by greed and dishonesty.

This was the mistake made by some of the explorers. They were greedy and cruel. In spite of that, however, the faith was planted in our land.

Studying New Words

channel	envious	rebellion
tribe	ascended	masts
conquer	water passage	independent
expedition	strait	retreat
fastenings	rigging	Pacific

Some Things to Do

1. On the map trace Pizarro's voyage on the Pacific Ocean. Trace also Magellan's voyage on the Pacific Ocean. Find the place where Balboa and his men discovered the Pacific Ocean.
2. Locate two discoveries of Magellan on his trip around the world.
3. Make a chart of all the Spanish explorers you have studied so far. Arrange your answers in three columns.

   1. Name of Explorer. 2. Land Discovered. 3. Waterway discovered.

4. Write the answers to the following questions:
   a. Who made a settlement on land called Panama?
   b. Who conquered the country north of the Isthmus of Panama?
   c. Who reached the new sea by sailing around a continent?
   d. Who conquered a country in South America?
   e. Who found a way to reach the East by sailing west?
   f. Which country became independent of Spain in 1821?
   g. When and where was the first college in the New World founded?

Things to Talk About

1. Tell how Cortes and Pizarro treated the Indians. Are they treated the same way today? Name other races besides the Indians to whom you can show Christian kindness.
2. Why was Pizarro killed?
3. With which explorer would you like to have traveled, Cortes or Magellan?

CHAPTER III

PATHWAYS IN THE SOUTHEAST

Early Pioneers of Florida. In this unit we have been studying about the great work of the Spanish explorers in America. We learned how they discovered the Pacific. We learned, too, about the first voyage around the world. These early explorers gave Spain more gold from Peru and Mexico than she ever hoped to receive from the Orient.

So far, in our unit, we have studied about lands which were south of the present United States.

This chapter is the story of Spain's pathways in the southeastern part of our own country. The story began with the search for a fountain of youth. It continued with a long search for gold. Spaniards explored the land which today forms the states of Florida, North Carolina, South Carolina, Virginia, Georgia, Kentucky, and Mississippi.

Missionaries went with each expedition sent out by Spain. These missionaries often gave their lives to spread the Catholic religion among the Indians. Even today, we can see signs of the Spanish heritage in America.

DISCOVERY ON EASTER SUNDAY

ONE of the Spaniards who came with Columbus on his second voyage was Ponce de Leon (pon'-thay day lay-own'). He settled on the island of Puerto Rico (pwer'-toe ree'-koe), and later became governor of the island.

One day, when he was quite old, he heard a strange story about an island to the north. The Indians told him there was a wonderful fountain of youth on that island. They said that those who drank its waters would never grow old.

Immediately Ponce de Leon set out to discover this wonderful fountain. He also hoped to find gold. He started north in 1513, the same year Balboa set out to discover the South Sea. When De Leon landed on the shore of the mainland of North America, his mind was set upon one thing. He must find the magic water, which would make him young again.

It was Easter Sunday. He saw beautiful plants and flowers on this land. This was truly a "Flowery Easter" for De Leon. That is why he called the land "Florida."

Although De Leon drank the water of many fountains and springs, he did not find the fountain of youth, nor did he find gold in Florida. Unfortunately for De Leon, this Indian tale was not true.

Second Visit to Florida. Eight years later, De Leon brought twelve missionaries to Florida in the hope of converting the Indians. He landed at **103**

a place which today is called Cape Sable. Soon after landing, however, De Leon was wounded in a battle with the Seminole Indians. His men took him to Cuba, where he died a few days later.

TRYING TO SETTLE FLORIDA

An Abandoned Colony. In 1526, another group of explorers started for Florida. These men set out from San Domingo with a leader named De Ayllon (day eye-lyown'). Three Dominican priests went with this expedition. Dominican priests live according to the rules that Saint Dominic laid down for them.

De Ayllon sailed farther up the coast than he had planned. He sailed as far as Chesapeake Bay, to a spot which today is called Cape Fear, Virginia. When he landed, De Ayllon started a settlement under the protection of Saint Michael.

The head of the Dominican missionaries was Father Montesinos (mon-tay-see'nos). He built a chapel and celebrated Holy Mass at this place in Virginia. Eighty-one years after this, some English people settled in Virginia. These Englishmen were not Catholics. Later in this book you will read about these English colonists. You must remember then that Holy Mass was offered in Virginia long before the English came to live there.

Shortly after the arrival of De Ayllon and his men, sickness broke out. The Indians also attacked the colonists. The Spaniards met so much trouble that they left the place and returned to San Domingo.

The Narvaez Expedition. About two years later, De Narvaez (day nar-vah-eth') set out to explore Florida. Several priests went with the expedition in the hope of converting the Indians.

De Narvaez and his men had to travel through swamps, and many of his men became sick and died. Besides, the Indians attacked the Spaniards again and again, and killed a great number of these explorers.

At last the whole expedition was wiped out. Only a man named Cabeza de Vaca (ka-bay'tha 105 day vah'-cah), and three companions remained alive. These four men were captured by the Indians, who made them slaves.

Finally, after eight years, De Vaca and his companions escaped. They wandered through the southeastern part of our country, went across Texas to the Gulf of California, and finally arrived in Mexico City.

They told about their capture and their long, hard journey. They said that there was a great deal of gold in the lands north of Mexico.

When the Spaniards in Mexico City heard about this, many of them decided to go in search of these riches. You will read about this search in the next chapter.

MARCHING THROUGH FLORIDA

HERNANDO DE SOTO (ehr-nan'-doe day soe'-toe) was a Spaniard who had become rich on expeditions to Mexico and Peru. Later, he went to Spain and spent his fortune foolishly.

De Soto returned to the New World, hoping to find riches again. This time he did not look towards Mexico, but towards the land north of Mexico and towards the east. He promised to give the King of Spain one-fifth of all the gold he might find.

De Soto started on his expedition with six hundred soldiers. Twelve priests also went along to convert the Indians.

The expedition set sail from Mexico, and landed on the coast of Florida a few weeks later. De Soto and his men started to explore the land. From Florida they went westward through swamps and woods. They crossed that part of our country which is now the states of Georgia, Alabama, and Mississippi.

The journey took so long that the priests used all the altar breads and wine they had brought along for the Holy Sacrifice of the Mass. Then they could no longer say Mass.

Many of the men died on this long, hard journey, but De Soto would not allow the others to turn back. It was during this part of the trip that most of the priests also died.

De Soto Is Cruel. During this journey, De Soto and his men met many different tribes of Indians. Instead of treating these Indians kindly, De Soto captured some of them and made them slaves. He bound them together two-by-two. He made them carry heavy loads of supplies. When he and his soldiers treated the Indians in this way they were not obeying Christ's law. What does Christ tell us about love towards our neighbor? Do you think the Indians were De Soto's neighbors?

De Soto Continues His Journey. A little later De Soto received a message that he was to give up his expedition and return to Spain. De Soto told the messenger that he would not return. He said he would find gold, or die in the forest looking for it. **107**

What does this story tell you about De Soto's character?

Two years passed, but still he found no gold. One day some Indians told De Soto about a great river called the "Father of Waters." De Soto made up his mind to find this river.

A Great Discovery. In 1541, De Soto first saw the waters of the great river. This was the Mississippi River, the "Father of Waters." The city of Memphis, Tennessee, stands today near the place where De Soto first saw the Mississipi.

De Soto and his men explored the land west of

the Mississippi River for many miles. More and more of his men became sick. Many of them died. De Soto himself fell ill and died the year after he discovered the Mississippi River.

The Spaniards were afraid that the Indians might attack them if they knew that De Soto was

dead. In order that the Indians might not find De Soto's body, his men buried him in the waters of the great river he had discovered.

The men who were still living prepared to sail south on the Mississippi. They made boats for themselves. Do you think this was an easy task? When the boats were finished, the men drifted down the river to the Gulf of Mexico.

Our Debt to De Soto. De Soto found no gold in all his travels. He found something more valuable than gold. He discovered the largest river in our country. It is one of the greatest waterways in the world. Of course, he did not know this. The Mississippi River is very important to us today. Can you give some reasons why it is important?

De Soto also did something for Spain. He gave that country the right to claim all the land east of the Mississippi. This land included the states of Florida, Kentucky, Georgia, Alabama, and Mississippi.

A Great Priest. We have read how the Spanish explorers were often cruel to the Indians and treated them as slaves.

We know, too, that priests usually accompanied the explorers on their expeditions. These priests tried to prevent the explorers from being cruel to the Indians. Many times the explorers would not obey the priests. The explorers were often cruel and greedy.

You know that God wants all of us to love our neighbors. Unfortunately, some of the explorers did not obey this law.

One of the priests who did a great deal to help the Indians was Father Las Casas. He was born in the New World, and was the first native of the New World to become a priest. He decided he would spend his life working for the Indians.

He often went to Spain and asked the King to

make laws that would prevent the explorers from making slaves of the Indians.

He also prevented people from being cruel to the Indians and treating them harshly.

The Indians loved him, and through him many Indians became good Catholics.

A MARTYR OF FLORIDA

Bound for Florida. Father Luis Cancer was a Dominican Father who converted many Indians in Central America. He wanted to carry the teachings of Christ to the Indians in Florida, even though the soldiers would not be there to protect him. Four other Dominicans went with Father Cancer to Florida.

Father Cancer chose a place to land where some Spaniards had landed before. These Spaniards had been cruel to the Indians. The Indians thought that all Spaniards would be cruel and unkind to them. They thought all Spaniards were their enemies.

The Martyrdom of Father Cancer. Father Cancer alone landed on the beach and prayed awhile. Suddenly the natives shrieked their war cry and jumped out from behind bushes and trees where they had been hiding. They rushed out and put Father Cancer to death. This event happened in the year 1549.

Those who remained in the boat saw Father Cancer in his agony. Arrows were shot at them too, but they escaped to Mexico. They told the story of Father Cancer's martyrdom to the settlers there.

Failure to Colonize. More attempts were made to settle in Florida. Each attempt met with failure. Then King Philip of Spain forbade anyone to try again. These trips cost too much money, and too many lives were lost. The King thought it useless to try to settle there.

THE OLDEST COLONY IN THE UNITED STATES

SHORTLY afterwards, some people from France planned to come to America. They settled on land that had already been claimed by Spain. These people were French Protestants. They arrived in 1562. This first attempt was not successful.

Again in 1564, French Protestants come to America. They settled in Florida, on the St. John's River, and established Fort Caroline there.

When the King of Spain heard that the French had settled in Spanish territory, he was displeased. He knew that the French were enemies of Spain, and could attack Spanish ships on the Atlantic Ocean. These ships carried valuable products from the New World to Spain. This made him change his mind about trying to settle Florida. He decided to make a settlement.

In 1565, King Philip appointed a man named Menendez (may-nayn'-deth) governor of Florida and made him commander of an expedition to that land. The King hoped that these colonists would stay in Florida and keep the French from taking the land from Spain.

On the feast of Saint Augustine (aw'-gus-tin) in 1565, Menendez arrived at a harbor in Florida. The colonists named their settlement St. Augustine. It was the first lasting colony established in what is now the United States. These colonists had priests with them, who said Mass for them and gave them the sacraments of our holy religion. We call priests who perform these duties *chaplains.*

Shortly after landing at St. Augustine, Menendez set out for the French fort. He marched **113** through swamps and woodlands until at last he found it.

Menendez captured the fort and put all the Frenchmen to death. He then left a few of his men to guard the fort, while he and the rest of his army returned to St. Augustine.

Tell why Menendez was wrong in what he did. Must Catholics always forgive their enemies?

MISSIONS FLOURISH IN FLORIDA

The Jesuits in Florida. In 1566, Menendez asked the Jesuits to come to preach to the Indians in Florida. Jesuit priests belong to a religious family known as the Society of Jesus. They take vows, as the Dominicans and Franciscans do, but they follow the rule of their founder, Saint Ignatius.

One of the Jesuits, named Father Martinez (mar-tee'-neth), was killed by the Indians soon after he arrived. Several other Jesuits came during the next six years. They traveled as far north as Chesapeake Bay. They tried to teach the Indians about Jesus Christ and the Catholic faith. Many of these Jesuits were martyred by the Indians. In 1572, the Jesuits left Florida to open missions in parts of Mexico.

The Coming of the Franciscans. The Franciscan friars came to Florida in 1577. They remained in Florida for almost two hundred years. They opened schools for the Indians. They learned to speak the Indian language. They taught the tribes to build their homes close to their missions so that the Spanish soldiers could protect them.

It was not easy to work among these Indians. They were very fond of their pagan ways, and did not want to give up their easy kind of life. Some of the Indian leaders made their people feel unfriendly to the Franciscans. These leaders said the Indians should keep their pagan customs and stay away from the friars.

A Dangerous Revolt. A dangerous revolt broke out in 1597. The son of one of the Indian chiefs had become a Catholic. Later, he turned against the Catholic missionaries. This man planned to kill all of the white men at one time.

The Spaniards were not ready for an attack, and five Franciscans were killed in a very short time. Some friendly Indians warned the other friars and the soldiers, who thus had time to escape. If the Spanish governor and his soldiers had not put down the revolt, the Florida missions would have been destroyed.

This revolt took place in a region of Florida called the Guale (gwah'lay) country. It is known as the Guale revolt.

Work of the Church. Florida was a part of the diocese of Cuba. In 1606, the bishop of Cuba came to Florida. He visited all the missions there. He also gave the sacrament of Confirmation to 2,000 Catholics, many of whom were Indians. The Kingdom of God was growing in the Land of Our Lady. **115**

There were many Catholics in America before settlers of any other religion came here to live.

The Franciscans sent more and more friars to the missions in Florida. As time went on, they built more and more schools. They did these things in spite of many difficulties, such as swampy land, unhealthy climate, and poor food.

Even though some of the explorers were cruel and greedy, the missionaries did the work of God. By 1688, there were 26,000 Catholic Indians in Florida, with thirty-five main centers. This period of history is known as the Golden Age of the Florida missions.

SLOW DEATH OF THE MISSIONS

LITTLE by little a change took place in the missions. It happened when the English, who were not Catholics, began to settle on the land that had been settled by Spaniards.

The English settlers tried to make the Catholic Indians give up their religion. Very often the English succeeded. They promised to trade with the Indians if they would not listen to the teachings of the friars.

The English did more than this to ruin Spanish Florida. They burned St. Augustine twice. In 1702 they destroyed many missions and settlements. They made slaves of the Catholic Indians.

Slowly the work of the Franciscans began to disappear. It died away because the English were moving in by degrees on the rich Florida lands.

In 1763, England got full control of Florida. Many friars and Spaniards had to leave because they were not free to practice their religion. Spain again got control of Florida in 1783, but the missions were not reopened. In 1819, Florida became the property of the United States. By this time the good work of the missionaries had disappeared. The English had ruined this vast mission field.

These missionaries did not come to Florida to seek riches or to become famous. They came only to save souls for Christ. Many of them became martyrs. That is, they gave up their lives for Christ. Others, who did not give up their lives, suffered great hardships and underwent severe trials.

It takes a brave man to undergo such hardships and trials.

These men helped to bring the Catholic faith to the New World. Although their mission buildings were later destroyed, and they themselves driven out, their work still remains.

Their example of goodness and holiness of life will never be destroyed. All Americans can learn from these brave men what it means to be true to God and true to country.

Learning New Words

abandon	vows	shrieked	relieve
drifted	chaplains	thrust	friars
violently			

Things to Remember

Two great discoveries; oldest colony in the United States; two religious orders in Florida; an early martyr of Florida; when Florida missions began to disappear; who saved the mission at the Guale revolt; two important Spanish explorers.

Working by Ourselves

1. Compare the size of Florida in De Soto's time with Florida today.
2. Name two Dominican priests mentioned in this chapter. Tell why their names are mentioned.
3. Prepare four sentences on why De Soto should have been just and kind to the Indians.
4. Select one of the explorers in this chapter. Write a paragraph about this explorer as though you were the explorer himself. Do not mention the name of the explorer. The title of your paragraph will be: "Who am I?" When you have finished, your teacher will ask you to read your paragraph to the class. Your classmates should then be able to name the explorer.

Discussing What We Have Learned

1. Give some reasons why the Spanish priests were martyred by the Indians.
2. If Florida had remained the property of the Spanish government, what language, laws, and religion would it have today?
3. Spain provided priests as chaplains for its soldiers. Does the United States do the same today for its soldiers? Explain your answer.
4. Why is it true to say that Catholics were in America long before the Protestant English settled there?

5. Why were the Indians cruel to Father Cancer?

CHAPTER IV

PIONEER TRAILS OF THE SOUTHWEST

Looking Over the Chapter. In the last chapter we saw how Spain claimed the southeastern part of what is now the United States. Other Spaniards were exploring the Southwest at the same time. They were searching for gold. Although they found no gold in the land we now call the United States, their explorations were of value. By these explorations they claimed the land for Spain. This land was more important than gold, although they did not think so then.

From Mexico, Spanish missionaries came to carry the Gospel of Christ to the Indians living in our land. Catholic priests worked for souls at Santa Fe (san'ta fay). These Spanish words mean *Holy Faith*. The Jesuits preached to the Indians in Arizona. Missions for Indians were opened in Texas. The first martyr in the United States died on the land of the great Southwest.

Many rivers, mountains, streams and valleys in the South bear the names of Christ and His saints. Many other places were dedicated to Our

Lady. This is only a little sign of the really big work the Spanish settlers did. They felt it was their duty to bring the religion of Christ wherever they settled. The mission schools and chapels of the Southwest were some of the means the Spaniards used to spread our holy religion in these lands.

CORONADO, THE EXPLORER

Reports of Seven Cities. Earlier in this unit you read about Narvaez. You learned how most of his men were killed by Indians. You learned that De Vaca escaped, and how he and his companions made their way to Mexico. He had heard that there were seven cities north of Mexico where the people were so rich that their houses were decorated with gold. These cities were called the Seven Cities of Cibola (see-boe'-la). De Vaca told the people in Mexico about these cities.

The governor of Mexico sent Father Mark, a Franciscan priest, to the north to find out if this story were true. A Negro servant, named Stephen, and Indian guides went with him. While on this journey, Stephen was killed by hostile Indians. The others returned without having seen any of the wealthy cities. They had heard more stories about these cities from the Indians.

The Long Search. Francisco Coronado was placed in charge of an expedition to the Seven **120** Cities of Cibola. Four priests and some friendly

Indians went with him. Indian servants drove cattle and sheep to provide food for the men during the journey. These were the first cattle to graze on the land we now call the United States.

Slowly Coronado's army marched through the North of Mexico. They captured the place now

called New Mexico. The Indians there told Coronado that the rich cities were farther on. This story was not true. The Indians told this untrue story because they wanted the white men to leave their land quickly.

Two of the Franciscan priests remained among the Indians in New Mexico to instruct them in the Christian religion. Later these Franciscans were killed by the Indians.

Coronado and his men continued on the journey. They came to a village of Indian dwellings. These dwellings were called pueblos (pweb'-loes). There was no splendid city to be seen, nor golden treasures to be found. This Indian village is believed to be in what is now the state of Kansas.

Father John of Padilla Is Martyred. Father John of Padilla (pa-deel'-ya) and two Brothers remained in this village to work for the Indians. Their work to save souls was very successful with this tribe of Indians. However, when they went to preach about Christ to the neighboring tribes, Father John of Padilla was martyred by them in 1544. He was the first martyr on the land which is now part of the United States.

After some time, Coronado gave orders to return. He was sad because he found no gold. However, during the three years of his search, he had explored much land for Spain. He had passed through the land which today is called Texas, Oklahoma, New Mexico, Arizona, Colorado, Kansas, and Arkansas. Some of his men had discovered the Grand Canyon of the Colorado River in 1542, and explored many other rivers. This was a great journey of exploration.

For almost three hundred years, this land belonged to Spain. Then, in 1803, the United States began to control parts of these lands. Today, all the lands explored by Coronado are part of the United States.

ALTHOUGH Coronado explored part of New Mexico in his search for the Seven Cities, he did not settle there. A colony was not established in New Mexico until 1598.

Don John of Oñate (owe-nya′-tay), a rich mine-owner in Mexico, led a band of soldiers and missionaries northward with a group of four hundred colonists. They crossed the Rio Grande River looking for a place to make their homes. They settled at Santa Fe about 1609. This colony was later to be the most important Spanish settlement in United States territory.

Farm Lands and Pasture Lands. The Spaniards found the rich soil of Sante Fe good for farming, so farming became one of their occupations. On the grassy plains of the land sheep and cattle grazed each day.

These settlers were happy as they tended their sheep and cattle and worked in the fields. They would gather in the evening for visits with their friends. Few visits were made back to Mexico. These people were citizens of a new land.

For two hundred years, New Mexico was a rather unimportant Spanish settlement. Many different tribes of Indians prevented the Spaniards from extending their little settlement, and raids upon them were frequent.

In the beginning only a few Indians became Catholics. However, after 1620, almost all of the **123** forty thousand Pueblo Indians became Catholics. Fifty Franciscans had worked among them in thirty missions throughout the length of the Rio Grande Valley.

Work of the Missionaries. Spanish priests opened the first schools in New Mexico to educate the Indians during the early days of the seventeenth century.

In 1670, there were many troubles in Sante Fe. Many of the Indians took sick because they had no food. The governor of the colony did not help them. Other tribes of Indians raided them. The Indians began to dislike the Spaniards because they did not help them in their trouble.

Among the Indians who were displeased with

the Spaniards was a leader named Popé (poe-pay′). He told the Indians they should give up being Catholics. He said they should live the way they did before the Catholic priests came. Popé also told these Indians that the religion of the Spaniards brought on their troubles. He made some of the Indians believe that they would be happier if there were no Catholic missions.

End of Mission. On August 10, 1680, a dreadful thing happened in New Mexico. This man, Popé, led the Indians in revolt. Twenty-one Franciscans were killed, and their missions were completely destroyed. The great work of many years was ruined in a very short time.

Who do you think suffered most from this revolt? Was it the missionaries who lost their lives? Would you say it was the Indians themselves?

Think about this question for a while. Your teacher will allow the class to talk about this topic later.

After twenty years, the Francsicans returned. The Indians who did not take part in the revolt welcomed back the Catholic priests. But very few of the pagan Indians were converted. They did not listen to the Spaniards. The days of the Pueblo missions were over.

There were still thirty-four Franciscans in New Mexico at the beginning of the nineteenth century. They began to take care of the spiritual needs of the white people who were settling there. **125**

The famous Santa Fe trail was opened in 1822. More Americans, with their American ways of living, were entering the settlement.

Mexico broke away from Spain in 1821. Then, New Mexico became a province of Mexico. When New Mexico became a part of the United States in 1848, there were no Indian missions left in New Mexico.

MISSONS IN ARIZONA

You read that in 1539, Father Mark explored the region north of Mexico. Part of that region is now the state of Arizona, but it was then a part of the land which belonged to Spain.

The Jesuit Missions. About 1690, a Jesuit named Father Eusebius Kino (you-see′bee-us kee′noe) came to establish missions in Arizona. He had only ten Indians for protection. Father Kino was very successful in this region. He traveled so much on horseback that he became known as the "horseback Padre." Some of his expeditions were eight hundred miles long, extending through the Santa Cruz (crooth) and San Pedro (pay′-droe) valleys. By these travels, Father Kino proved to the Spaniards that California was not an island, as they had believed at first.

After his death, Father Kino's work was continued by other members of the Society of Jesus, until 1767. At that time, the Jesuits had to leave 126 all the Spanish missions, through orders from the

Spanish government. The Franciscans came to take over the work in Father Kino's mission field.

Father Francis Garces (gar'-thes) was the leader of the Franciscans in this field. He was very successful in teaching the Indians about our holy faith. The Spanish soldiers, however, were treating the Indians very cruelly. The missionaries tried to stop the soldiers from mistreating the Indians. But the soldiers refused to obey the priests. The Indians rebelled against this harsh treatment. They rose up against the Spaniards and put many of them to death. Among those who were killed was Father Garces. Even though he was a good friend to the Indians, they put him to death. This revolt occurred in 1780, in the land we now call Arizona.

Many priests left this region, because Arizona became a territory of Mexico when that country became independent of Spain. When the United States took over this region in 1848, Catholic Indians were still found among the mountains of Arizona. Arizona became a state of the Union in the year 1912.

MISSIONS IN TEXAS

EARLY Spanish explorers had passed through the land between the Sabine and Rio Grande Rivers. It was here that the French explorer, La Salle, landed in 1585. He lost his way looking for the mouth of the Mississippi and landed in Texas by accident. While he was in Texas, he built a fort, which he called Fort St. Louis.

When the Spaniards heard that the French had established Fort St. Louis on their land, they did something about it right away. The Spanish King sent some soldiers to destroy the settlement. When they arrived, they found nothing but an empty fort and deserted homes. The Indians had destroyed it only a short while before they arrived. Later we shall read about La Salle.

At this same place, the Spaniards set up a fort of their own in 1690. The Franciscans were placed in charge of this mission settlement.

About this time, two Spaniards asked an Indian the name of his tribe. He replied "Tejas" (tay´-has), which means "friends." After that, the land was known as Texas, the land of friends.

Famous Mission Schools. Several colleges were started in New Spain to prepare Franciscan priests to do missionary work. One of the most famous colleges was founded by Father Anthony Margil (marg´-heel). He also set up a mission in San Antonio, and spent many years converting the Indians in Texas.

The Franciscan mission at San Antonio later became the center of the Spanish government. Some soldiers came to live in it. These soldiers belonged to the division of the Spanish army known as the Company of the Alamo (al´-a-moe). So the building came to be called the Alamo. When

128

you study about Texas later in United States history, you will learn more about this famous building.

Missions in Texas continued until about 1830. They were not so successful as in other places. There were few converts to the faith. At the end

of the eighteenth century, there were only three thousand Catholics in the whole of the great land of Texas. The white people who settled became numerous, and the Indians wandered about from place to place.

Texas belonged to Spain until 1821. Then it became the property of Mexico. In 1836, it became independent of Mexico, and in 1845 became a state of the United States. By this time, there were no Indian villages left in Texas.

Catholics in Texas. The Spanish missions in Texas brought the faith to the Indians who lived there. They also kept the faith alive among the Spanish people who settled there.

Even to this day, there are many Catholics in Texas. Outside the city of San Antonio there stands one of the first missions built in that part of the country. It is on the grounds of a seminary where priests are trained.

In this great land, many places are named after saints. For example, San Antonio is named after Saint Anthony. The city of Santa Fe is named after our holy faith, for Santa Fe means "Holy Faith." These things show how the explorers often thought of God and the saints.

Finding Important Facts

1. Find on the map the land explored by Coronado. Prepare to discuss with members of the class the exact location of the Spanish colony founded in that section; also, the mission centers in that area.
2. From Chapters III and IV name three famous explorers and two colonizers. Tell also why each of these Spanish explorers is important.
3. Hold a history quiz on this chapter. Compose three questions which you will ask your classmates. If none of your classmates can answer your question, you must be prepared to give the correct answer.

Talking Over Our Problems

1. De Soto and Coronado found no gold in the south-

ern section of our country. Why, then, do we say that their explorations were important?

2. Does the Church ever force people to become Catholics? Suppose a tribe of Indians heard all about Jesus Christ and did not believe He was the Son of God. What would Catholic missionaries do then?

3. Why were some Spanish missionaries killed by the Indians? Can you tell why Father Cancer was martyred in Florida? Who martyred Father John of Padilla?

4. Which discovery was more important, that of de Soto or of Coronado? Give a reason for your answer.

New Words to Study

pueblos	Alamo	canyon
revolt	Cibola	conversions
disease	John of Padilla	relief
dedicated		displeased

Connecting the Stories of the Chapters

1. On a sheet of paper, fill in the spaces in the chart below. First, reread the chapters of this unit and the preceding one, if necessary.

Explorer	Native Country	Country for Which He Sailed	Discovery of Land	Present Owner
a. Columbus				
b. Magellan				
c. Pizarro				
d. Cortes				
e. Dias				

2. Select one explorer who traveled through land that is now owned by the United States. Trace his path on the map. Mark his most important discoveries.

3. Name all the priests you studied about, who were martyred in the United States.

131

CHAPTER V

WHERE THE MISSION BELLS RING

Looking Over the Chapter. Long ago, a brown-clad Franciscan came to California. He tied a bell to the branch of a tree and rang the bell so that everyone in the neighborhood could hear it. Then he waited to see what would happen.

Soon one lone Indian appeared. The kind priest gave him a present, which the Indian treasured. Then the Indian left. He came back with some of his Indian friends. Father Serra, the Franciscan priest, taught the Indians to pray.

Ever afterwards, when the mission bell rang, the natives answered the call and came to pray with Father Serra. Before long, the bells of twenty-one mission churches rang in California. You will read in this chapter about this saintly priest and the many ways in which he made God known and loved in California.

THE COMING OF THE PADRE

Three Countries Want the Same Land. Spain had several claims on the land called California. As early as 1542, a Portuguese explorer named John Cabrillo (ka-breel'-yo), explored part of the western coast of the United States. He said that people called the land California.

Many years later, in 1599, a Spanish merchant was looking for a port of shelter on the western coast. He finally anchored his ship in a bay on the coast of California.

Spain was not the only country which had its eyes set on California. Far towards the north was Russia. Russia owned Alaska and was anxious to have the land farther down the coast also. This land was California.

Another country which was anxious to have California was England. One of her explorers, Sir Francis Drake, once landed there. You will read more about Drake later in this text.

Spain Has a Plan. Spain was determined to own this land. She decided to send a large group of soldiers there to protect it from other countries. But they found that the cost of a fort and an army would be too great.

Another plan was agreed upon. Spain would send missionaries from Mexico to the Indians. A few soldiers would be sent along to protect the missionaries.

Father Junipero (whoo-nee'-pay-roe) Serra was placed in charge of the Franciscan Fathers, who came to California in 1769. The group settled at San Diego.

Purpose of the Missions. The Indians in California had never heard about God and His great love for them. Father Serra wanted to help them in every way. He and his missionaries would teach the Indians how to save their souls, to love and serve God well.

Besides knowing nothing about the one, true God, these Indians had a very uncivilized way of living. They did not know how to build suitable homes for themselves. They did not know how to cultivate the land.

Father Serra planned to build missions for these Indians. At these mission settlements, the Indians could be taught how to till the soil, build homes, and live as true Christian people. Father succeeded very well.

Father Serra knew that the land in California belonged to the Indians. When they were able to take care of their own lands, he intended to divide the lands among them.

PORTS OF PEACE

ON JULY 16, 1769, Father Serra arrived at San Diego. He celebrated Mass at the foot of a cross overlooking the harbor at San Diego. This was a good place to make a settlement, for there was plenty of water, good soil, and timber.

After six months, many kinds of hardship visited the group of missionaries. Disease and famine covered the land. The Indians became unfriendly and cruel. There were very few supplies left for the missions.

These troubles upset the soldiers of the establishment so much that their chief officer, Portola, thought it better to return to Mexico. Father Serra begged him to remain for at least nine days more. In the meantime, Father Serra prayed and prayed to God for help. Still there were no signs of help. Father Serra prayed on.

At sunset on the ninth day, a ship was seen on the horizon. It was bringing food and help. Father Serra's prayer was answered. The mission was saved. This was the beginning of the great mission system of California.

Soon after this, Father Serra began the first mission building, which had thick adobe walls, and beautiful Indian and Spanish paintings.

More Indian Missions. In June of the following year, a mission was established at Monterey. His second mission was the place where Father Serra lived until his death.

The third mission is named after Saint Anthony of Padua. In Spanish it is called San Antonio de Padua. Part of this old church has been repaired so that Franciscans still go there now and then to celebrate Holy Mass.

On September 8, 1771, Father Serra founded a mission in honor of Saint Gabriel the Archangel. It is usually called by its Spanish name, San Gabriel.

Two priests came from San Diego to start this mission. As soon as they arrived, Indians appeared with spears, bows, and arrows. The Indians intended to fight the Spanish priests. The brave missionaries put their trust in God and prayed for help. The Indians came closer and closer. The

priests had with them a beautiful painting of our Blessed Mother. They unrolled it before the threatening Indians.

A strange thing happened. The Indians stood still, as if someone had cast a spell over them. They laid down their bows and arrows. Then they became friendly with the missionaries, and even helped them to set up their mission bell on an oak tree nearby. What made the Indians change their minds about the priests?

Although each mission had a belfry, the belfry tower at San Gabriel was especially beautiful. It was different from the belfries of other missions because it had an outside stairway. This mission

is so beautiful it has often been called "Pride of the Missions."

Troublesome Times. Four missions were now built. In 1772, however, things were not going well at these missions. The Indians burned San Diego and killed one of the missionaries. There were few converts. There was very little money for the most necessary supplies. The only food and equipment the missionaries could receive came from Mexico in small sailing vessels that landed in California.

Father Serra was once again afraid that the governor of Mexico would close the missions and send the priests back to Mexico. Father Serra tried to prevent this.

He set out to travel 2400 miles to Mexico. When he reached that country, he explained the good that was done by the missions. He asked for more money, more settlers, more missions. He wanted the government to build a road through California, so that the settlers could get their food and other articles more quickly than by sea.

Father Serra won the day. He got everything he wanted. Thanks to the prayers and pleadings of saintly Father Serra, the missions were saved.

THE SPREAD OF THE MISSIONS

The Valley of the Bears. The next mission was often called the "Valley of the Bears," because there were many bears in that part of the country. The mission was dedicated to Saint Louis, who was a holy bishop. It was called Mission San Luis Obispo (san loo'-ees o-bees'-poe).

The first four missions had thatched roofs which could easily catch fire. The San Luis mission was the first to have a tile roof. Every mission after San Luis also had a tile roof.

138

San Francisco's Oldest Church. The mission dedicated to Saint Francis of Assisi was the only church in San Francisco for seventy-five years. This mission still reminds the people of San Francisco of the glories of early mission days. However, the repaired church is no longer used for church services.

Father Serra's Chapel. The seventh mission has the name of a Spanish saint, John of Capistran. The Spaniards called it San Juan Capistrano (san hwan cap-ees-tra'-no). It is also called Padre Serra's Chapel. The first adobe church, in which the saintly Father Serra celebrated Holy Mass and baptized souls, is still standing.

The Swallow's Song. Spring is a happy time at the Capistrano mission. Hundreds of swallows nestle beneath the eaves of the church, and sing their joyous songs. Then the young swallows begin to take their flying lessons. Summer rolls on, until one day late in the season, the swallows become very noisy. If you understood bird language, you would know they were getting ready to leave Capistrano. Suddenly they rise and fly towards the South.

The swallows leave in October each year, around the feast of Saint John Capistrano. They return about March 19th of the following year.

A mission dedicated to Saint Clare of Assisi was the eighth one founded by Father Serra. Three churches have since been built on this spot, but **139** they were destroyed by earthquakes or floods.

The last mission which Father Serra built was named after Saint Bonaventure. Like so many of the other missions, it was destroyed later. Another church was built in its place in 1809.

A HOLY HERITAGE

FATHER SERRA died on August 28, 1784. He was then seventy years of age. He was quite tired and worn out from traveling back and forth between the missions. At his death, there were five-thousand converts among the Indians in California.

Father Serra's statue was placed among the statues of other outstanding men in the Capitol building at Washington, D. C.

A heritage is anything that is passed on to us from our ancestors. The heritage that Father Serra left to America is a holy and sacred one. For six hundred miles along the coast of California he left his chain of missions, each one only a day's journey from the previous one. The road upon which these missions were founded is called the "King's Highway." This highway was dedicated, not to any earthly king, but to Christ, our Heavenly King.

Mission Work Continues. The work that Father Serra began was continued by a Franciscan named Father Lasuen (la-soo-ayn'). Next, the Santa Barbara mission was built. The Franciscan priests still have charge of this mission. It also has a very valuable library, containing many priceless books and documents.

In all, Father Lasuen built nine missions. Three more were constructed after that. These completed Father Serra's chain of twenty-one missions.

Destruction Follows. The glorious mission days came to an end early in the nineteenth century. This change came about when Spain broke away from Mexico in 1821. Then Mexico began to rule California.

The Mexicans were very dishonest in their

dealing with the Indians of California. They robbed them of all their lands and property. They stole the precious and valuable articles that belonged to the Indian missions.

The mission buildings themselves were not kept in order or repair. By 1834, there were no more Indian missions in California.

In 1840, California was made a diocese. Bishop Diego was its first bishop. He came to live at the Santa Barbara mission.

Mission Restored. Ten years afterwards, California became part of the United States. Some of the people in the United States were anxious to have the Spanish missions restored. They wanted them to look the same as in the days of Father Serra. Many people in the United States gave large donations for this purpose. The missions were restored as closely as possible to the Spanish style in which they were built. Have you ever visited these historical places?

With Saddles and Sandals. In this unit you read about the travels of the Spaniards in America. You learned that the kind missionaries came with the Spaniards to preach the Gospel and teach the Indians. These missionaries established the first mission schools in our land. The Spanish language, culture, and customs are still with us in the lands settled by the Spaniards long ago.

Another heritage left to us by the Spanish in the great Southwest is the Catholic religion. The

Spanish missionaries traveled through this great region, and everywhere they went they left churches and schools.

In these schools the Indians were taught how to cultivate the land. They were taught about our faith and how to be good Catholics.

The Spanish missionaries were doing the work that God wanted them to do.

It was the Son of God, Jesus, who said that His followers were to go and teach all nations all things which He had commanded.

Words to Make Your Own

horizon	adobe	belfry
tile	thatch	San Antonio
donations	equipment	documents
uncivilized	heritage	

Can You Answer These Test Questions

1. Why is Father Serra's statue in Statuary Hall, Washington, D. C.

2. Compare Father Serra's treatment of the Indians with that of De Soto.

3. Turn to the map on page 128. Make a list of all the missions found along the King's Highway.

4. Why did Spain send Catholic missionaries to California?

5. Who paid for the rebuilding of the Spanish missions as they are today?

Studying the High Lights of the Unit

1. What is the title of this unit? Do you think this is a good title? Give your reasons.

2. Name all the explorers who made discoveries on the two continents of the western hemisphere. Make three columns on your paper and write above them the following headings:

   Explorer   Discovery   Owner of Land Today

3. Continue the time-line begun in Unit I. Your teacher will give you the most important dates of this unit which you may illustrate on your time-line.

4. Name the priest who did most to free the Indians from slavery; the great missionary of Texas; the martyr of Florida; the first martyr of the United States; the great friar of California; the priest who said Mass in 1526 on present Virginia land.

5. Locate on the map the following places:
   a. Where the oldest colony in our land was founded
   b. The second oldest colony in our land
   c. The country of North America where the Spaniards found gold
   d. The land where Father Kino labored
   e. The King's Highway
   f. Father Margil's missionary field
   g. The first settlement on the mainland of America
   h. Route of the first voyage around the world
   i. Balboa's trip to reach the Pacific Ocean
   j. Land where Pizarro found gold
   k. Section where Father John of Padilla was martyred; where Father Cancer was martyred

UNIT TWO — MASTERY TEST

I. Number lines on your paper 1 to 20. On each line write the correct answer to one of the following questions.

1. The country directly south of the United States is _____.

2. Peru is on the continent of _____.

3. Florida is on the continent of _____.

4. The _____ Ocean lies on the eastern coast of our land.

5. The two largest oceans in the world are connected in South America by the _____.

6. The Philippine Islands are surrounded by the _____.

7. An isthmus is a narrow neck of _____ connecting larger portions of _____.

8. The land explored by De Soto and Coronado is now part of _____.

9. The Strait of Magellan leads to the _____ from the eastern shore of South America.

10. St. Augustine is located in _____.

11. The conqueror of Peru was named _____.

12. The first martyr of the United States was _____.

13. Father Antonio Margil labored for many years in _____.

14. The Mississippi River was discovered by _____.

15. The Aztec chief in Mexico was called _____.

16. _____ reached the East by sailing west.

17. The oldest colony in the United States was
_____.

18. _____ discovered the Pacific Ocean.

19. The saintly founder of the California missions was _____ _____.

20. The Grand Canyon was discovered by _____.

II. Number lines on your paper 1 to 10. After each number place the letter that is before the correct answer in each item below.

1. The Pacific Ocean was first discovered by
   a. sailing around the Cape of Good Hope
   b. crossing the Isthmus of Panama
   c. crossing land in the United States
   d. sailing south from Panama

2. The voyage of Magellan proved that
   a. Columbus had not found a New World
   b. the tale of the Indian was true
   c. Columbus had not reached the Indies
   d. the land Cortes discovered was Mexico

3. Which of these events happened first?
   a. the discovery of Florida
   b. the first settlement in the United States
   c. the first voyage around the world
   d. the discovery of the Pacific Ocean

4. The most successful Spanish missions in the United States were:
   a. missions at Sante Fe
   b. those established in the lands of Texas
   c. those in California
   d. missions in Kansas

5. De Leon's expedition was important because
   a. he found gold on the land he discovered
   b. it was the first settlement made in Mexico

146

    c. it was the first discovery on the main-
   land of the Americas

    d. it was the first discovery on United
   States soil

6. Peru and Mexico are called treasure-houses of
   Spain because

    a. the explorers brought wealth to these
   countries

    b. Spain built treasure-houses in those
   countries

    c. the explorers sent gold and silver to
   Spain

    d. Spain spent so much money on these
   expeditions

7. The oldest colleges and universities in the
   New World lay in

    a. the land called the United States

    b. land south of Peru

    c. land south of the United States

    d. Española

8. The land explored by De Soto is that located
   in

    a. the Southwest of the United States

    b. Panama

    c. the Southeast of the United States

    d. the southern part of South America

9. Spain was the first country to explore the
   New World because

    a. no other nation wanted to explore a new
   land

    b. her sailors were better trained than
   others

    c. the King of Spain wanted the Spaniards
   to conquer the Indians

    d. Columbus claimed the land for Spain
   when he discovered it

10. The land explored by Cortes is today the property of
    a. Spain
    b. United States
    c. Mexico
    d. Panama

III. Number lines on your paper as usual, 1 to 10. After each number write the letter that answers each statement correctly.

1. Belfry means
    a. something on the water
    b. clerk
    c. bell-tower
    d. balcony

2. Mainland means
    a. main island
    b. land and water
    c. middle of the ocean
    d. the chief land

3. Galleon means
    a. a place where prisoners are kept
    b. horse and cart
    c. ship
    d. soldiers

4. Expedition means
    a. to show how things work
    b. some men going out to explore
    c. to go some place on water
    d. a try-out

5. A pueblo is
    a. a straw hut of the Indians
    b. a wigwam

      c. an Indian village

      d. a cabin built by the Indians

6. Revolt means

      a. to commit crime

      b. to turn against someone

      c. to guide someone

      d. robbery

7. Adobe means

      a. Spanish house

      b. a kind of cement

      c. sun-dried bricks

      d. a kind of Spanish hat

8. Epidemic means

      a. a shot of medicine

      b. a disease that spreads rapidly

      c. a petition for a favor

      d. a gold rush to the West

9. Horizon means

      a. a hill

      b. the sun comes up

      c. the place where earth and sky seem to meet

      d. the setting of the sun

10. New Spain means

      a. The United States and Canada

      b. Mexico

      c. South America

      d. Panama

IV. Place the correct letter after each number on your paper.

  1. When Father Serra gave the Indians presents, he did so because

      a. He was afraid they would not be kind to him if he did not.   **149**

b. He knew the Indians needed these articles.

c. He wanted to be kind to the Indians, so that they would be kind to him.

d. He knew the Indians were his brothers, because God is our Father.

2. When Menendez destroyed the French fort, he killed all the men. What do you think of this act?

a. He did what was right because the Spaniards owned that land.

b. The French had a right to settle there and should not have been killed.

c. He did what was right because the French were his enemies.

d. He should not have punished the French by killing them.

3. Pizarro killed the Inca chief because he was afraid he would be killed by him later. What should Pizarro have done? Should he have

a. kept him prisoner?

b. freed the Inca, and kept his promise?

c. returned all the gold to the Indians, but kept the Inca prisoner?

d. killed the Inca?

4. Father Serra spent his life working for the Indians in California. What was his chief reason for doing so? Was it because

a. he liked to work among the Indians?

b. he received a large salary for doing this work?

c. he wanted to be famous later on?

d. he wanted to serve God and teach the Indians to do so, too?

5. Father John of Padilla stayed in Kansas instead of returning to Mexico with Coronado. What do you think of this?

   a. He should have returned with Coronado.
   b. He stayed there because he loved the wilderness and savage tribes.
   c. He did not like traveling around with explorers.
   d. He stayed there because he loved God and wanted to save souls.

V. Fill in the blanks below with either one of the following phrases, whichever is correct.

   a. practicing charity
   b. dealing honestly and justly

1. The Inca chief kept his word to Pizarro. In doing this he was ＿＿＿＿＿＿＿.
2. Father John of Padilla was kind to the Indians. By this he was ＿＿＿＿＿＿＿.
3. De Soto was unkind to the Indians. He knew he should have been ＿＿＿＿＿＿＿.
4. The Mexicans robbed the missions. They were not ＿＿＿＿＿＿＿.
5. The Spanish missionaries taught the Indians many things. By their acts they were ＿＿＿＿＿＿＿.

VI. Answer the following questions on your test paper. Make complete sentences.

   a. What two great deeds did the Spanish missionaries and explorers do for the United States?
   b. What kind of treatment did Montezuma receive from Cortes?
   c. Since the Spaniards first settled Florida, why is it not owned by Spain today?
   d. Tell what is meant by the expression, "The King's Highway."

Our Lady

of

Lourdes

Pray for us

PRAYER

O VIRGIN Immaculate, Mother of God and my Mother, from thy sublime height turn upon me thine eyes of pity. Filled with confidence in thy goodness and knowing full well thy power, I beseech thee to extend to me thine assistance in the journey of life, which is so full of dangers for my soul. And in order that I may never be the slave of the devil through sin, but may ever live with my heart humble and pure, I entrust myself wholly to thee. I consecrate my heart to thee forever, my only desire being to love thy divine Son Jesus. Mary, none of thy devout servants has ever perished; may I too be saved. Amen.

(Indulgence of 500 days. S.P. Ap., May 17, 1919 and April 29, 1935).

UNIT THREE

FOR SOULS AND SABLES

CHAPTER I —NEW FRANCE BEGINS

Fishing waters around Newfoundland.

Verrazano and Cartier explored lands for France.

Cartier discovered the St. Lawrence River.

The first permanent French colony was founded in 1608.

The French settled in Maine.

The French founded Acadia.

Champlain explored the Iroquois country and land around Lake Huron.

The French founded Montreal.

CHAPTER II —AMONG THE MISSIONS

The Jesuits opened missions among the Hurons.

Eight Jesuits were martyred in North America by the Indians.

The Jesuits converted the Huron Indians.

The Jesuits opened missions in Maine and Acadia.

Father Sebastian Rale was martyred in Maine.

153

The English tried to make the Catholic Indians give up their faith.

The Indians of Maine remained loyal to the Catholic religion after missionaries were forced to leave.

CHAPTER III—FROM LAKES TO GULF

The French explored the land around the Great Lakes.

French Missionaries established missions in this land.

Nicolet thought he would reach China.

Missions and fur stations were erected around Lake Michigan and Lake Superior.

The French heard tales of a great river.

Father Marquette and Joliet explored the Mississipi as far as the Arkansas River.

The French explorers returned to their homes.

The Jesuits established many missions for the Indians.

La Salle was a French nobleman who came to New France.

La Salle and his men crossed Lakes Erie and Michigan.

Father Louis Hennepin was captured by the Indians and discovered the Falls of St. Anthony.

La Salle sailed the Mississipi to its mouth and claimed it for France.

UNIT THREE

FOR SOULS AND SABLES

A Rival Nation. After Spain had begun to explore America, other nations in Europe joined the race for lands and riches. This unit tells how the French came to the New World. It tells how they explored lakes, streams, and rivers in the search for souls and sables. Sables are beautiful black furs from a little animal called the sable.

Spain had settled lands in the South of the United States. France entered lands north of the United States, in the land we now call Canada. France did not build many colonies in this Land of Our Lady. Her people came chiefly for purposes of trade, not to make America their future home.

The French brought their language and customs to our land. Most of all, they helped spread the Catholic religion.

Catholic missionaries went wherever the French trappers went. The natives had the Gospel of Christ preached to them. One entire Indian tribe was converted through the teachings and labors of the French missionaries. The Indians called these priests "Blackrobes." During a war **155** between two Indian tribes, eight of the priests on the Indian missions suffered martyrdom for the love of Christ.

The French were usually friendly with the Indians. Only one group, the Iroquois (ear'-oh-kwoy) Indians did not become friendly with the French people.

France claimed much land in America. She claimed land around the Great Lakes, and around the Mississipi River. Quebec in the north, and New Orleans in the South were hers, but the principal French colony was Quebec.

In this unit we shall read some more stories of bravery and sacrifice. We shall read of the founding of two great cities that lie to the north of our own land. These cities are in Canada.

But greater than the founding of cities was the work done by the French in helping to bring the Catholic faith to the New World. As in the case of the Spanish explorers, missionaries came with the French explorers. These missionaries also came to convert the Indians and to spread a knowledge of God. Some of them gave their lives for this purpose.

We shall also read about some great discoveries which had a great effect on the history of our own country.

Although France no longer owns land in America, her explorers and missionaries have left **156** us a great heritage.

CHAPTER I

NEW FRANCE BEGINS

Looking Over the Chapter. Visitors to Canada enjoy the scenes in Quebec and Montreal. Thousands of Catholic people from the United States make pilgrimages to the shrines and churches of these cities each year. Can you name two of the famous shrines in Canada?

Although France does not rule Canada today, the people of Quebec and Montreal speak the French language. We shall learn why this happened. In 1608, a great French leader led a band of colonists to the place where the St. Lawrence River turns into a narrow stream. This man was Samuel de Champlain (sham-plain').

The story of early days in New France tells about Champlain and his dealings with the Indians. When he died, Quebec was a thriving colony. It was the first French colony in the New World.

EXPLORING FOR FRANCE

Fishing Grounds in the North. Far towards the north, off the Atlantic coast, there is a large island called Newfoundland (new-found'-land). Not long after Columbus' discovery, fisherman from France and England visited this island. Cod, herring, mackerel, and other kinds of fish were found in the waters around Newfoundland.

These fishermen made a living for themselves and their families by making frequent trips to Newfoundland. These trips also made them familiar with the land around Newfoundland. They became interested in these lands.

Sailing along the Coast. The King of France wanted his country to get some of the new lands in America. He was anxious to have one of his sea captains discover a passage through the continent. He hoped that this would open up a new route to China. In 1524, King Francis I empowered Verrazano, (ver-ra-tsah'-no), an Italian, to command an expedition to the New World.

Verrazano started by sailing South from France. Then he turned westward and sailed across the ocean to the southeastern shores of what is now the United States. He sailed up along the coast until he reached Labrador, but he found no passage to China. From Labrador, he returned to France. His voyage was a very important one for France. Because of Verrazano's voyage, France claimed the land along the coast.

Discovering a Waterway. Ten years passed before King Francis I sent another expedition to **158** America. This time it was a fisherman, Jacques

Cartier (zhak car-tee-ay′), who set out to find a waterway to China. No river runs from the East to the West across North America. But in 1534 no one in Europe knew that. Cartier turned his two ships in the direction of Newfoundland. This place was well known to all French fishermen.

After sailing along the northern and western coasts of Newfoundland, Cartier came upon a large bay, or gulf. He called it the *Gulf of St. Lawrence* because it was discovered on the feast day of that saint. Can you find this Gulf on your map? Can you find the date of this feast day on your calendar?

South of the Gulf of St. Lawrence at a place called Gaspé (gas-pay′), Cartier went ashore. He and his men set up a large wooden cross bearing the coat of arms of the King of France. By this act, he claimed the land for France.

Since winter was near, Cartier returned to France. In his report to the King he said that the waters were rich in cod, herring, mackerel, and other kinds of fish.

In the spring of the following year, Cartier came again to the land. This time he sailed up the river which is called the *St. Lawrence*. This was in 1535. On the way he met several friendly Indians. Sometimes Cartier would ask these Indians the name of a place through which he was passing. The Indians always answered "Canada," which is an Indian name for *village*. Some people think **159** that this is how Canada got its name. When we speak of Canada today, we do not mean a little village, but rather a large country directly north of the United States.

As Cartier sailed up the river, he thought he was on the way to China. But instead of China he came to steep waterfalls. These waterfalls pre-

vented his boats from going farther. He still believed that he was on the way to China, so he gave the waterfalls the French name for China, which is "La Chine" (la sheen). Do you know how far away China is from La Chine?

Near the waterfalls was a large mountain **160** which Cartier called "Mont Real" (monh ray-al'), or "Royal Mountain." Today the great city of Montreal is located at this spot.

Cartier returned down the river and went ashore at a place now called Quebec (kay-bec'). This was a place where the Indians had many fine furs of animals they had trapped. Cartier knew these furs were very valuable and he wanted some furs to take back to France. He spent the winter

at Quebec in order to bargain with the Indians for these furs. During the winter many of Cartier's men took sick and died. When spring came, the few men who had not died during the winter returned to France, carrying with them the furs they had gathered.

FOUNDING A COLONY

Early Attempts That Failed. In 1541, Cartier

made another voyage to the New World. This time he tried to found a colony. But he did not succeed. The colonists were not accustomed to the hard work necessary to found a colony. They gave up their plans for a colony and went back to their quiet, peaceful farm life in France.

In 1603 a group of Frenchmen tried to settle in Acadia. There were many Catholics among this group, and two priests came with them as chaplains. We shall learn later that the English also claimed this land. Because they felt the land was theirs, they attacked Acadia. In 1654, it was completely destroyed.

The French also began a settlement in what is now Maine. Jesuit priests came along as chaplains, and as missionaries to the Indians. This colony did not last long. The English claimed that the land belonged to England, and they destroyed the work of the French. They either sent the missionaries back to France or left them to perish. Other settlers came, but they, too, suffered from an English attack in 1654.

A Colony at Last. Among the colonists who came to Acadia, there was a young Frenchman named Samuel de Champlain. He was interested in the lands of the New World. He made up his mind to spend his life exploring and colonizing for France.

In 1608, he and a band of French colonists

sailed up the St. Lawrence River to the place

where Cartier had spent the winter many years before. Here at the foot of a great rock, Champlain founded his colony. He called it Quebec. "Quebec" means "narrowing of the stream." This was the first permanent French colony in the New World.

Three buildings and a storehouse were immediately erected. These were surrounded by a wall made of long, pointed logs, called a palisade. The palisade had loopholes for guns and platforms for cannon. It was like a fort.

A Hard Winter. During the first winter the colonists did not have enough food, and many of them died of starvation. Because of the cold weather, only eight colonists remained alive. In the spring, more colonists arrived. With Champlain as leader, Quebec became a thriving colony. Because this great leader began the first French colony in America, he was given the title, "Father of New France." New France was the name given to the French lands in America.

FRIENDS AND FOES OF CHAMPLAIN

Friendly Indians. Champlain soon became friendly with the neighboring Huron (hyou'-ron) Indians by trading with them. He exchanged valuable animal skins for articles that had been brought from Europe.

Champlain was a very good Catholic, and wanted the Indians to know and love God. In 1615 he brought Franciscan priests to New France. **163**

These French Franciscans are called *Recollects*. They came to teach the Indians about God and the Catholic religion. Ten years later Champlain sent to France for some Jesuit priests to help the Franciscans. The Jesuits dedicated their first mission to Our Lady of the Snows. Champlain, from the very beginning, set about spreading the Catholic religion in New France.

Champlain's Mistake. Because Champlain was a friend of the Hurons, they asked him to take part in a war against the Iroquois Indians. The Iroquois were a group of five Indian tribes. The most famous of these tribes was known as the Mohawks. They lived south of New France in the land we now call New York State, between the Hudson River and Lake Erie.

Champlain took part in this war against the Iroquois, but later he was very sorry he did. Champlain killed many of the Iroquois with his guns and cannon. Ever afterwards, they remained the enemies, not only of Champlain, but also of the entire French people.

It was a mistake for Champlain to treat the Indians this way. It is against the law of God for us to be cruel to others, even if we do not like them. We should obey God's law.

The Iroquois would not trade with the French. They always took sides against them in time of war and kept the French from gaining control of

lands to the south of Canada. What do you think

of the way the French treated the Iroquois? Give reasons for your answer.

TRAVELS OF CHAMPLAIN

WHILE Champlain was fighting the Iroquois he traveled through much of the land around Lake Erie. He learned the best route into the Iroquois country. He discovered a beautiful lake in

northern New York. We call it Lake Champlain. Find this lake on your map.

In Huron Lands. Between 1613 and 1616 Champlain explored the lands where his friends the Hurons lived. He sailed up the beautiful Ottawa (ot'-a-wah) River and then traveled by land to Lake Huron. This route became the great highway for the French fur traders for nearly one hundred years.

At the northeastern corner of Lake Huron, Champlain reached a spot called Georgian Bay. Here he found a Franciscan, Father Le Caron (car-on'), living among the Hurons and teaching them the Catholic religion.

While traveling in the land of the Hurons, Champlain discovered the waters of Lake Ontario.

Many trading posts were built along the Indian trails. Here beads, bells, ornaments, or colored balls were exchanged for the costly skins of the beaver, otter, and mink. Sometimes the French would trade cheap articles for valuable furs. Most of the French preferred this kind of trade to planting crops and making their homes in the New World.

Do you think they were wise to do this?

CHAMPLAIN IN QUEBEC

The Captured Colony. Just when the little colony of Quebec was getting along well, a great misfortune happened. In 1628 a large fleet of English ships sailed up the St. Lawrence River to attack the settlement. Champlain knew he could not defend the colony against the English. He decided to surrender immediately. The English gained control of the colony. They sent Champlain to England as a prisoner, and ordered the priests to return to France.

The Return of Champlain. Four years later, Quebec was given back to the French, and Champlain returned to govern his colony. In thanksgiving to God for saving Quebec, Champlain had a chapel built on a nearby mountain.

The Jesuit priests returned to their Indian missions in 1632.

Death of Champlain. Champlain died in 1635. The people of New France were very sad at the death of their leader. He gave France her first permanent colony. He gained for the French the friendship and trade of the Huron Indians. Through him, Franciscan and Jesuit missionaries came to work in New France.

A Catholic School in Quebec. In 1639, some Sisters arrived from France. They were called the Ursuline Sisters, which means that they chose Saint Ursula as their special saint. The Ursulines came to teach school in Quebec. Which saint is the patron of the Order or Community of Sisters who teach in your school?

The Ursulines were the first to open a Catholic school for young girls in New France. From that time on, the daughters of French colonists could get a Catholic education in New France.

MONTREAL IS SETTLED

The Great Fairs. The French bought Montreal from the Indians in 1642. It became famous as a great fur-trading center. Frenchmen set out from

Montreal to build distant trading-stations and to explore farther into the wilderness.

These French traders also encouraged the friendly Indians to gather skins and load their canoes with them and bring them to a fair held in Montreal. This fair took place in the spring. Sometimes over a thousand Indians came. They brought many, many skins! This shows that the Indian hunters and trappers were very skillful.

Then the trading would begin. The French had such articles as beads, blankets, kettles, powder, guns, bullets, and brandy, which had been brought from France. Although these articles had no great value to the French, they traded them with the Indians for their animal skins worth hundreds and hundreds of dollars. Do you think this was a fair trade or an unjust deal? Why?

The Indians stayed at Montreal for some time before returning to their homes. Do you know what highway the Indians used to go home?

As winter came on, the trapping season began again. The Indians liked to gather furs in winter because the animal skins were thicker and heavier in winter than at any other time.

Catholic Priests Come to Montreal. In 1644, some Catholic priests came to Montreal and built schools for the French and Indian children. These priests were members of the Society of Saint Sulpice (sul-pees'). They are called Sulpician (sul-pish'-an) Fathers.

The chief work of the Sulpicians is to train young men to become priests. They began this work in Montreal by building a seminary in 1663. A seminary is a special school for boys who want to study to become priests. Ever since that time, the Sulpicians have had a seminary in the city of Montreal.

Can You Fill in the Blanks?

Below is an outline of the chapter just studied. Copy this outline in your notebook. Then, *without rereading the chapter,* fill in the blanks as you go along. After your teacher has corrected your work, you may have to reread certain sections of the chapter. *Always write full sentences.* The words written in parenthesis below are intended to help you over the difficult spots, but they are only hints to the correct answer.

I. **Exploring for France**
    A.—————————— (Along the coast)
    B.—————————— (A northern river)

II. **Founding a Colony**
    A.—————————— (Early attempts)
    B.—————————— (First permanent colony)

III. **Friends and Foes of Champlain**
    A.—————————— (Indians friendly to Champlain)
    B.—————————— (Champlain's mistake)

IV. **Travels of Champlain**
    A.—————————— (Land explored and lake discovered in Iroquois country)
    B.—————————— (Highway for fur traders—lake discovered)

V. Champlain in Quebec

    A.————————————(Event of 1628)

    B.————————————(Work of Champlain in city)

VI. Montreal is Settled

    A.————————————(Why Indians came to Montreal)

    B.————————————(First seminary in Montreal)

Some New Words to Learn

Find these words in the chapter and see if the rest of the sentence helps you to understand the meaning of each word.

palisade	fur trader	community
dedicated	martyrdom	Recollect
wilderness	permanent	Sulpician
trading post	seminary	

Lest We Forget

1. Begin a new time-line with this unit. Insert the dates of the French explorations. Follow the same plan as in Unit I.

2. Study well the map on page 160. Each place located on that map has some connection with this unit. If you cannot recall these place-names, review the chapter so you will receive a high rating on the mastery test later.

3. Contrast Champlain and Cortes as leaders.

4. Tell whether you think all the French people in Canada should have had to suffer because Champlain went to war against the Iroquois.

5. Give an account of what happened at the French trading posts.

CHAPTER II

AMONG THE MISSIONS

Looking Over the Chapter. When Champlain fought with the Hurons, the Iroquois were defeated. The Iroquois hated the Hurons so much that they decided to put an end to the entire Huron tribe. Such unkindness is directly against Christ's command that people and nations love one another. The missionaries tried to teach the Indians this command of God. Why do you think the missionaries were not always successful?

The Iroquois attacked the Huron villages. During these raids they killed eight of the Jesuit priests who were living among the Hurons. By this time the Jesuits had converted the entire Huron tribe. So, although the Iroquois killed their enemies, many of the Hurons died as Christians, children of God, and heirs to the kingdom of heaven.

The Jesuits also opened missions among the Iroquois. These were not so successful as the Huron missions. Many of the Indians would not become Catholics; others, however, became very good Catholics. One of the converts was a saintly little girl known as the "Lily of the Mohawks." Did you ever read a story about this Indian girl?

In Maine, Capuchins (cap′oo-shins), Sulpicians, Franciscans, and Jesuits worked among the Indians. Even after the priests were driven from Maine by the British, the Indians remained true to the Catholic religion and would not become Protestants.

ON THE HURON MISSIONS

WHEN the Jesuits came to the Huron missions in 1625, they converted these Indians to the Catholic faith. News of the "Blackrobes'" work spread even to the Illinois Indians, who invited the Jesuits to come to them. The Jesuits could not grant their request because they had only enough priests to attend to the Huron missions.

Martyrs in New York. The most famous missionary to the Hurons was Father Isaac Jogues (zhog). He came from France in 1636. He stayed at Quebec a short while to learn the language and customs of the Indians. Father Jogues spent the next six years among the Indians around Lake Ontario and the St. Lawrence River valley.

In 1642, Father Jogues went to Quebec to visit the headquarters of the Indian missions. This was a nine-hundred-mile journey from his little mission. He made the trip by canoe and on foot. Along

172

with him went René Goupil (reh-nay′ goo-pil′), a French doctor, who had been working among the Indians.

On the return trip, they met a band of Mohawk Indians. You remember, the Mohawk Indians were unfriendly to the French. The Indians captured both the priest and the doctor. They were

taken to the Iroquois country. Because of this capture, Father Jogues was the first Catholic priest to enter New York state.

While Father Jogues was a prisoner, the Iroquois tortured him cruelly.

They killed René Goupil by splitting his head with a tomahawk.

They beat Father Jogues until he was almost dead. The Indians tore out his fingernails and chewed off some of his fingers. These are only a few of the ways in which the Iroquois tortured Father Jogues.

Father Jogues finally escaped from the Iroquois and received help from some Dutch settlers at Albany. They helped him to leave the country and go to France.

A Martyr's Privilege. A priest is usually not allowed to offer the Holy Sacrifice of the Mass if he cannot hold the Sacred Host in the thumb and forefinger of each hand. When Pope Urban VIII heard how Father Jogues' hands had been mangled, he immediately gave Father Jogues special permission to offer Holy Mass even though parts of his fingers were missing.

These are the beautiful words of the Pope to Father Isaac Jogues: "It would be shameful that a martyr of Christ should not drink the Blood of Christ!"

Father Jogues loved the Iroquois even though they had tortured him. He wanted to go back to New France to help the Indians. At last, in 1644, his superiors allowed him to return.

Two years later, Father Jogues was sent by the French to the Iroquois to make peace with them. A young man named John Lalande (lahland') went with him. Father Jogues succeeded

in making peace. On his way back to Quebec a

band of roving Indians attacked him and his companion. This happened at Auriesville, New York. Both Father Jogues and John Lalande were killed by the tomahawk. A chapel now stands at the place where they were martyred.

The War Continues. Carrying the guns given them by the French in trade for furs, the Iroquois entered the land of the Hurons in 1648 and raided their villages. One morning during this war, Father Daniel had just offered the Holy Sacrifice of the Mass in his Huron mission chapel when the Iroquois attacked. After he was pierced and stabbed with many arrows, they threw his bleeding body into the flames of the burning chapel.

In 1649, Father John Brébeuf (bray-beuf'), the superior of the Jesuit priests, was burned by the savage Iroquois. Boiling water was poured over his head in mockery of baptism. He was so brave in his sufferings that, after his death, the Indians ate his heart. They thought that this act would make them as brave as he. They did not know that Father Brébeuf was brave and good because he had the powerful help of Almighty God. Father Gabriel Lalemant (lall-mant') was killed in the same way on the following day.

Father Charles Garnier (gar-nee-ay') and Father Noel Chabanel (shab-a-nel') also suffered martyrdom in 1649. Pope Pius XI proclaimed these eight martyrs "Saints of the Catholic **175**

Church" in 1929. The church celebrates the feast of these martyrs on September 26.

Love Proved by Kindness. After the Iroquois raids, only a few Hurons remained alive. The French brought these Hurons to live on the protected banks of the Ottawa River. This meant the Indians could no longer trap for furs, and sell them to the French. The French lost a good in-

come. Even though they lost money, the French willingly made this sacrifice to help their suffering Huron neighbors.

AMONG THE IROQUOIS

In 1654 the Jesuits opened a mission for the Iroquois at Lake Ontario. It was a most difficult and dangerous work, but the French government sent soldiers with the Jesuits as protection. The Hurons who were held captives by the Iroquois were glad to see the missionaries and receive once again the grace of the sacraments.

Not many of the Iroquois became Catholics. Because of the constant dangers on this mission,

the Jesuits built villages for the Indians near Montreal. They invited the Catholic Iroquois Indians to come to live there. Many of those who went there lived lives of great virtue.

One of those who went to live near Montreal was a saintly Mohawk girl named Kateri Tekakwitha (kat′-er-ee tek-ak-with′-a). She was born at

Auriesville, New York, ten years after Father Jogues was martyred there. For her pure and pious life she received special graces from Almighty God. She is called "Lily of the Mohawks." She died at La Prairie, near Montreal, in 1680.

End of the Iroquois Mission. The English became powerful friends of the Iroquois in 1680. By 1688 war between France and England had started, and the Jesuits had to leave the Iroquois lands. Can you tell why?

MISSIONS IN MAINE AND ACADIA

ALTHOUGH the French were driven from their settlements in Maine and Acadia, small groups of them returned later. In 1632, the Capuchin Fathers came to Maine, where they set up missions and established schools.

The young Indian converts were taught to bring the knowledge of God to their own people. This work came to an end in 1654, when the English captured twenty-three priests and nine brothers and sent them back to France.

After this, the Indians of Maine often traveled to the St. Lawrence River valley to visit the Catholic missionary priests. In 1688, the French sent missionaries to this land again. The Jesuits came to the Abenaki (ab-e-na'-key) Indians along the Kennebec River.

The Indians were glad to see these priests and treated them with great respect.

A Martyr in Maine. The Abenaki land was claimed by both the English and the French. Some Indians began to attack the English settlers and raid their villages. Father Sebastian Rale (ral) was a Jesuit who served for many years on the Indian missions. He was wrongfully accused of setting the Indians against the English. The English seized this aged missionary and murdered him on August 23, 1724.

After Father Rale's martyrdom, the Abenaki Indians were left without a priest for eighty years. The English tried hard to make them accept a Protestant minister, but they firmly refused to give up the Catholic faith. Instead, they often traveled three hundred miles to Quebec to go to confession and receive Holy Communion. The loyalty of these Indians makes us realize how much they appreciated the Catholic religion brought to them by the Jesuits.

The story of these Catholic Indians, who traveled many miles to go to Mass should make us think about our lives.

We have an easy time going to Mass. Usually we do not have to go very far. In many cities the church is a few minutes' walk from home.

And yet, we often go to Mass only on Sundays and holydays. We should try to go oftener, every day if possible.

The faith of the Indians should teach us that the Holy Sacrifice of the Mass is so great that we should attend it as often as we can. If we go to Mass, we should also try to go to Holy Communion every time we go to Mass.

Improving Your Vocabulary

loyalty	tomahawk	successful
enemy	Auriesville	tortured
torment	merited	captive
superiors	income	

To Make You Think

1. In what way did the French practice charity to the few remaining Hurons?

2. Whom do you admire more, the Indians of Maine or the Lily of the Mohawks?

3. Why did the Iroquois put the missionaries to death?

4. Discuss ways in which God blessed the work of the Jesuits among the Hurons and the Iroquois.

5. Name an Italian girl canonized in 1951, who was pure and holy like Kateri Tekakwitha.

Things to Do

1. Find in your classroom library some stories about the French missionaries. Write a short composition on the one you like best.

2. Tell the class why you think Father Jogues deserved special permission to say Holy Mass.

3. Which do you think is more pleasing to God, to die a martyr like St. Isaac Jogues, or to die after living a holy life like Kateri Tekakwitha?

CHAPTER III

FROM LAKES TO GULF

Rivers and Lakes. Champlain never went farther west than Georgian Bay on Lake Huron. However, fur-trading posts sprang up farther west along Lake Michigan and Lake Superior. Missionaries followed to set up missions for the Illinois Indians.

The Indians told about a great river not far away. This news brought great hope to the hearts of the French. They thought that perhaps this was the waterway to the West. If this great river flowed into the Pacific Ocean, they thought, then a short water route to China soon would be found!

The governor of New France sent a young man and a Jesuit missionary to find this great river about which the Indians spoke. When these explorers discovered that it emptied into the Gulf of Mexico, they knew this was not the waterway that led to China.

Later a brave French adventurer named La Salle obtained permission to explore this river from the Great Lakes to the Gulf of Mexico. He tried to found a colony at the mouth of this river, but failed. Soon afterward, he was wounded by one of his followers, and died.

La Salle claimed the entire Mississippi Valley for France. He called it Louisiana territory after the French King Louis. France lost this land later. It has since been divided to form several states of our country.

FRENCH EXPLORE THE GREAT LAKES

Early Settlements. One of the men who traveled with Champlain was named Nicolet (nee-co-lay'). He was a fine hunter and knew the Indians well. In 1634, the Hurons asked Nicolet to travel westward, to make peace with a tribe of Indians with whom they wished to be friends. The Hurons called these Indians "People of the Sea."

Nicolet was happy as he prepared for the journey. From the description the Hurons gave him, he thought the place where he was going must be near China. So, in his supplies for the journey he carried a finely embroidered green garment of Chinese style. He intended to wear this if he should meet some Chinese in the land of these People of the Sea.

Nicolet found the Indian tribe. He made peace with them in the name of the Hurons, but he saw no Chinese. Do you know why not? He was exploring land at Green Bay, Wisconsin, on Lake Michigan!

A French settlement was made on the land between Lake Superior and Lake Michigan in 1641. It was called Sault Ste. Marie (soo sant ma-ree'). A little later a missionary post was established at St. Francis Xavier, Green Bay, Wisconsin. Can you find these places on your map?

An Indian Mission. Father James Marquette (mar-ket') was one of the Jesuit priests who came to the Indians around Lake Michigan and Lake Superior. He erected a mission chapel near the Strait of Mackinac, which connects Lake Huron and Lake Michigan. This mission was named St. Ignace (ee-nyass') in honor of Saint Ignatius, the founder of the Jesuits.

From his mission Father Marquette visited other Indian tribes around Lake Michigan.

In Western Lake Superior. Daniel du Luth (du-loot'), explorer and fur trader in New France, set out for adventure along the western shore of Lake Superior. He was always kind to the Indians with whom he lived and traded. He knew that they were God's children. This made him treat them as his brothers, for he knew that he too was a child of God.

Du Luth set up his fur station at the place in Minnesota which is now called Duluth.

WILL THE GREAT RIVER LEAD TO THE PACIFIC?

Tales of a Great River. From time to time word had come to Father Marquette's mission about a river which the Indians called "Missi Sipi." This **183**

means "great river." The French people wondered if this river could possibly empty into the Pacific Ocean or whether it flowed directly south.

We must remember that at that time the lands south of Lake Superior and Lake Michigan were an unknown wilderness to the white men. The French fur traders became very much interested in this great river.

The governor of New France appointed a fur trader named Louis Joliet (jo-lee-eh'), and the Jesuit missionary, Father Marquette, to explore this great river. They were to discover into which body of water it really flowed.

In preparation for this journey, Father Marquette learned six Indian languages. He wanted to be able to talk with the Indian tribes along the way, so he could bring the Word of God to them.

The Journey South. On May 17, 1673, Father Marquette, Louis Joliet, and five other men, in two birch-bark canoes, set out on Lake Michigan. They headed for Green Bay and the Fox River. When the Fox River became too shallow for them to go farther, two kind Indians showed them the path

by land to the waters of the Wisconsin River. This path over which they carried their canoes and supplies is called a *portage*.

Father Marquette often stopped along the banks of the Wisconsin to preach to the Indians. He sometimes smoked the peace pipe with them as a sign of friendship.

Each day found the explorers farther and farther away from their homes in the North. They slept on the shore each night, because it would have been dangerous to travel on unknown waters in the dark.

The exploring party sailed along the Wisconsin River until June 17, 1673. Then they came to the clear waters of the Mississippi River. Father Marquette was overjoyed at the glorious sight. Since he had a great love for the Blessed Mother, he wanted to honor her every way he could.

That is why he named this great waterway after her. He called it "River of the Immaculate Conception."

When the small band of explorers started down the Mississippi, they found the current swift and strong. The river ran southward, sometimes in zigzag fashion but always towards the south.

Soon the explorers found another large river whose muddy waters joined the Mississippi from the west. The Indians nicknamed this river "The Big Muddy," but we call it the Missouri River. This river is a branch, or tributary, of the Mississippi River.

A little farther south, Father Marquette and Joliet saw another river emptying into the Mississippi. This river came from the east. It is called the Ohio River. As Father Marquette and his companions went farther south, they found the Ar-

kansas (ar'-kan-saw) River. Father Marquette

and Joliet stopped at this spot. They saw no need of going any farther. They learned from some Indians that the river flowed on to the south.

The Answer Is Found. The French explorers had done their work well. The governor of New France sent them to discover into what body of water the Mississippi River flowed. Now they knew the answer. The Mississippi River did not flow into the Pacific Ocean. It went steadily south into the Gulf of Mexico.

This was the same river De Soto had discovered for Spain many years before. Now, because of their trip as far as the Arkansas River, the French also claimed the Mississippi.

The French explorers knew they were on dangerous ground. The Spaniards and the Indians might attack them at any moment. They were afraid to go any farther south. So they turned their boats around and started home again.

The Return Journey. The trip up the Mississippi was not easy. The men had to paddle their canoes against the current. After some time, they reached the spot where the Illinois River empties into the Mississippi. Here Father Marquette and Joliet parted from each other.

Joliet planned to travel to Quebec to tell the governor about this trip. Father Marquette went back to his mission at St. Ignace, using another route than the one he explored on the journey down the Mississippi.

Father Marquette sailed up the Illinois River. Perhaps no white man had ever before sailed up this river. Along the way, he stopped and preached to the Indians. He often smoked the peace pipe with them, and promised to come back again to them soon.

From the Illinois River, Father Marquette sailed on and on until he finally came to Lake Michigan. The next stop was his mission home, St. Ignace.

Father Marquette came back to the Indians along the Illinois River twice afterwards. He founded a mission for these Indians, and named it the Immaculate Conception Mission.

During his stay at this mission, Father Marquette became ill. He died on his way back to St. Ignace.

Honor to Father Marquette. There is a special room in the Capitol building at Washington called Statuary Hall. This room contains statues of people of the United States who did great service to our country. In 1895, the state of Wisconsin placed the statue of Father Marquette in this hall. By doing this, the state honored him as one of its greatest men.

Can you give some reasons why?

CHIEF OF THE RIVER FARERS

In 1660, a young French nobleman named
Robert de la Salle (sal) came to New France. He

lived for a while on a large estate which he owned, but he preferred to travel about and seek adventure. Soon he became a trapper, roaming here and there through the forests of New France.

From Trapper to Explorer. After about ten years of this kind of life La Salle made up his mind to go exploring. He wanted to sail the Mississippi right down to the Gulf.

La Salle obtained permission from the French King to try out his plan. Fifty men prepared to go with him. A few Franciscan priests also went along. One of these priests was Father Louis Hennepin (hen'-e-pin). We shall read more about him later in this book.

A man named De Tonty was chosen as La Salle's helper. Sometime before this, De Tonty had fought in a war in Europe. De Tonty lost one of his hands at that time. In its place he wore an iron hand. Because of this, the Indians nicknamed him "Tonty of the Iron Hand."

The first thing La Salle did was to build a fort on the shores of Lake Ontario. He called it Frontenac, in honor of the governor of New France. A little farther south, he built another fort at Niagara (nye-ag'a-ra). One of the priests stayed at this fort to give the white men and Indians all the blessings of our holy religion. Can you tell some of the duties of this priest?

The Lost Ship. La Salle had a large ship built, which he called the *Griffin*. The Indians had never **189**

seen such a ship as this before. It had great white sails and plenty of room on deck. It was the first ship ever to sail the Great Lakes.

After a swift sail on Lakes Erie and Huron, the *Griffin* stopped at different places on Lake Michigan to trade with the Indians. In a short time the ship was overloaded with furs. La Salle sent the *Griffin* back to Lake Erie to unload these furs, get more supplies, and sail back again to Lake Michigan This ship sailed away, and was never heard of again.

In the meantime, La Salle and the men who remained with him, crossed Lake Michigan by canoe. On the southern bank of the lake, they built Fort St. Louis. Then La Salle went down the Illinois River to the place now called Peoria (pee-o'-ree-a).

Here Indian guides began to desert La Salle, and his men begged him to turn back. La Salle refused. Instead, he built a fort here and called it "Crevecœur" (crev-cur'), which means "heartbreak." La Salle decided to leave all but five of his men here, under the command of De Tonty, Then La Salle and his five companions started the long, hard journey back to the Great Lakes to get more supplies.

Exploring in Chains. Before leaving, La Salle ordered a group of men to explore the land farther south, below Crevecœur. Father Louis Hennepin, 190 a Franciscan priest, was head of this group. Some

Indians belonging to the Sioux (soo) tribe at-tacked the white men on this trip and made them prisoners. This event caused the white men to do far more exploring than they had planned.

First, the Indians took Father Hennepin and his men down the Illinois River to the Mississippi. Then they rowed up the Mississippi. No white man had ever been on this part of the river before. Even though the French were prisoners, they were exploring for France!

Quite a distance up the river, the red men and the white men met some waterfalls or rapids. Father Hennepin named them the *Falls of St. Anthony*. They are in the state of Minnesota. Beside these rapids now stands the large city of Minneapolis.

On the next day, Du Luth made a journey up this part of the river. He was one day too late to be the first explorer of this region. But Father Hennepin's men were glad to see Du Luth. He helped them to escape from the Sioux Indians. You can imagine how fortunate these men were.

Father Hennepin went to France afterwards and did not go with La Salle on the rest of the journey.

At the Gulf. In the meantime, La Salle had learned that his ship, the *Griffin,* was lost. What do you think happened to the ship?

But still worse news was to come. La Salle received a message that the Indians had raided 191

Fort Crevecœur and destroyed it. Some of the French escaped to the north. Just as soon as the Indians left, the French came back to Crevecœur.

La Salle was still determined to explore the Mississippi. He got supplies ready, and early in 1682 set out on the Illinois River. He and his companions soon were on the broad waters of the

Mississippi. They passed the spot where Marquette had turned back.

La Salle at the Gulf. In all, four months went by before La Salle finally reached the Gulf. There he set up a pillar on which was written: "Louis the Great, King of France, rules here, April 9, 1862." By this act he claimed all the land for France. Besides the French and Spaniards, could anyone else claim this land?

La Salle gave the name Louisiana to all the land surrounding the Mississippi. The map on page 160 will give you some idea of the size of this land.

A SOUTHERN SETTLEMENT

AFTER this voyage, La Salle went to France and gave the King an account of this journey. He asked the King to establish a colony at the mouth of the great river. La Salle was afraid the Spaniards might make a settlement there. If they did, none but the Spaniards could use the Mississippi River.

The French Failure. The King of France thought it was a good thing to settle in the South. Before long, four ships with four hundred colonists set sail from France. La Salle was the leader. He had a different route in mind this time. La Salle planned to sail across the Gulf of Mexico until he found the mouth of the river.

It was easy to reach the Gulf of Mexico from the Atlantic Ocean. However, La Salle had trouble in finding the mouth of the river. His maps and charts were not correct.

La Salle lost his way. He went too far west on the Gulf of Mexico. He turned back a short distance, but still had no success. A landing had to be made somewhere. This landing took place on the shore of Texas, only three hundred miles from the **193** actual mouth of the Mississippi. The colonists built a fort called St. Louis.

Shortly after this landing, La Salle was killed by one of his own followers. He was one of France's greatest explorers.

The little band of French colonists did not last long in Texas. In Unit Two you read about the terrible thing that happened after they landed. Do you remember what happened?

New Orleans Begins. Soon afterwards, the French again tried to settle at the mouth of the river. Two small French settlements were made along the Gulf. In 1717, the French succeeded in making a settlement at New Orleans. This was just what La Salle had planned, but failed to do. La Salle's dream was coming true.

The first group to settle at New Orleans were not the kind of men who make good colonists. They did not want to work and put up with hardships. After awhile, other colonists came who were good workers, and did much to build up the little colony. The French settlement around New Orleans was to become one of the most important parts of the United States.

Priests in Louisiana. In those early days, the Catholic bishop of Quebec was also the bishop of all Louisiana. The Capuchin Fathers were given charge of all the French Catholics from the southern part of Louisiana to the Ohio River. In the 194 whole Mississippi Valley, however, there were never more than twenty priests at one time.

The Jesuits had charge of all the Indians in Louisiana. However, they did not make so many converts in the South as they did in the St. Lawrence River valley.

Catholic Schools in the South. The Capuchin Fathers started a Catholic school for boys in New Orleans seven years after the city was founded. The Ursuline Sisters opened a Catholic school for girls in 1727. Their pupils learned sewing, knitting, and fine needlework besides reading, writing, and arithmetic.

These Sisters were the first to teach in a Catholic school on United States soil. They still have an academy for girls in New Orleans. Later, these Sisters opened an orphanage and a hospital in New Orleans. They worked among the rich and poor, Indians and Negroes.

Louisiana's Flags. The French flag continued to wave over Louisiana for about eighty years. In 1763, the French flag came down. Two other flags followed it. The English flag waved over the land on the eastern bank of the river, and the Spanish flag arose over the land on the western bank. Only the land on the west of the river kept the name Louisiana.

The flag of the United States of America was raised over Louisiana Territory in 1803. By degrees, the land was divided into states. The first formed from that territory was named Louisiana. **195**

Visitors to New Orleans today find there many things to remind them that the French first settled there. The language, manner of living, and the customs of the French still remain among many of the people of the Mississippi River valley.

Catholics in Louisiana. The heritage of Louisiana is a Catholic heritage. We have just read about the early explorers, especially La Salle, who was a good Catholic.

We have seen how the faith was planted in this land.

Today there are many churches throughout Louisiana and the people are faithful to the teachings of the Catholic Church.

New Words to Learn

portage	territory	Crevecœur
accurate	Peoria	estate
tributary	current	Statuary Hall
course	Sioux	

Map Game

Your teacher will help you play this game. Below are ten different things to do. You must first study them well. In a box, your teacher will place ten slips of paper, each with a different number on it. When your teacher calls your name, you will draw a number from the box and find that number below. Then answer the question and show the location of the place on the wall map.

1. Tell about the journey of Nicolet. Trace his journey.

2. Locate Du Luth's fur station.

3. Name and locate two settlements on the Great Lakes.

4. Find the source and mouth of the Mississippi River. Give explorer of each.

5. Show where Joliet and Marquette started on the Great Lakes.

6. Name the tributaries of the Mississippi passed by Marquette and Joliet.

7. Show the place where Marquette and Joliet halted on the Mississippi.

8. Trace La Salle's voyage from Fort Crevecœur to the Gulf of Mexico.

9. Show the class the path of Father Hennepin and the Indians.

10. Trace the voyage of La Salle from the Chicago River to the Gulf of Mexico.

Points for Study and Discussion

1. Why was Father Marquette's statue placed in the Capitol at Washington?

2. Show the difference between the discovery of De Soto and that of La Salle.

3. Tell why France came to the New World.

4. Who do you think was braver, La Salle or Cortes?

5. Find out when the community of Sisters who teach you opened their first school in the United States.

A Good Way to Review

Compare the colonists of Spain and France in America. Show in what ways they were alike and how they differed from each other. Compare their reasons for coming to America; where they settled; the success they had; how they treated the Indians; the religion they practiced; and their language.

Construct a large time-line, combining material learned in Units 2 and 3.

Essentials of the Unit

1. On an outline map of the United States, fill in the region explored by the French.

2. Write on your paper the names of all the French explorers you read about in this unit.

3. Your teacher will divide the class into groups, and give each group the name of one French explorer. Each pupil in each group will then write three sentences about its explorer. These sentences must tell the most important things about the explorer.

UNIT THREE—MASTERY TEST

I. Fill in these blanks by writing the answers on another sheet of paper.

1. Sault Ste. Marie is between Lake ＿＿＿＿＿ and Lake ＿＿＿＿＿.

2. A fur trader named Du Luth settled on Lake ＿＿＿＿＿.

3. The Falls of Saint Anthony are near the present city of ＿＿＿＿＿.

4. Champlain founded a colony on the ＿＿＿＿＿ River.

5. Cartier spent a severe winter at ＿＿＿＿＿.

6. Mission St. Ignace is situated between ＿＿＿＿＿ and ＿＿＿＿＿.

7. Verrazano explored the Atlantic Coast from ＿＿＿＿＿ to ＿＿＿＿＿.

8. Saint Isaac Jogues was martyred at ＿＿＿＿＿.

9. The French claimed lands as far west as Lake ＿＿＿＿＿.

10. La Salle's colony landed at a place in_____.
11. The Jesuits opened an Iroquois mission at Lake _____.
12. The Abenaki Indians lived in _____.
13. La Salle wanted to found a colony on the Gulf of _____.
14. Georgian Bay flows into Lake _____.
15. Father Hennepin explored the _____ northward from the Illinois River.
16. The French explored Lakes _____, _____, _____, _____ and _____.
17. On his first voyage, Cartier explored the Gulf of _____.
18. Joliet explored the Mississippi River as far as _____ River.
19. Father Le Caron labored among the_____ Indians.
20. The Indians along the Illinois River heard about God through the preaching of _____.

II. A. Match the following. Write the answers on your paper.

Explorer	Place Explored
1. Verrazano	( ) Lakes to the Gulf
2. Father Hennepin	( ) Quebec
3. La Salle	( ) Mission St. Ignace
4. Champlain	( ) Carolinas to Labrador
5. Father Marquette	( ) Falls of St. Anthony
	( ) Iroquois country

B. Do the same with the following:

Catholic Missionaries	Place
1. Father Le Caron	( ) Maine
2. Father Rale	( ) Quebec
3. Ursuline Sisters	( ) Montreal
4. Sulpician Fathers	( ) Georgian Bay
5. Saint Isaac Jogues	( ) New Orleans
	( ) New York

III. Select the correct answer which explains each term and write it on your paper.

1. The "course" of a river is
   a. where the river ends
   b. that part of the river that moves swiftly
   c. its path
   d. the mouth of the river

2. A "palisade" is
   a. a theater
   b. a wall of long, pointed logs
   c. a building like a palace
   d. a group of forts

3. "Rapids" are
   a. strong waves caused by the wind
   b. rocks in the streams and rivers
   c. that part of the river where the water flows swiftly
   d. stony streams

4. A "portage" is
   a. a place where ships come in and go out
   b. a ship headed for port
   c. carrying goods overland from one river to another
   d. a small port on a river

5. A "current" is
   a. the flowing of the river
   b. the air flowing over a body of water
   c. wind coming from different directions
   d. a cool breeze on the water

IV. Number lines on your paper 1 to 20. After each write the answer to the following questions, "Yes" or "No."

1. Were the Spaniards in America before the French?

2. Did Cartier look for a passage to China?

3. Were the Mohawks one of the Iroquois tribes?
4. Did Champlain fight the Hurons?
5. Were the Hurons converted by the Jesuits?
6. Were the French looking for gold mines?
7. Did the Catholic Iroquois come to Montreal?
8. Was Father Rale murdered by the Indians?
9. Was Father Marquette the first Catholic priest to enter New York state?
10. Was Nicolet the earliest French explorer around Lake Superior?
11. Did the English destroy early French settlements?
12. Were the French the first to discover the mouth of the Mississippi?
13. Did La Salle give the name Louisiana to the Mississippi Valley?
14. Was Kateri Tekakwitha a Huron maiden?
15. Do the French own the Mississippi Valley?
16. Were the Jesuits called Blackrobes?
17. Did the Ursulines come to New Orleans?
18. Was Joliet's voyage important?
19. Did the English claim Louisiana?
20. Did the Spanish claim Louisiana?

V. Answer these questions in complete sentences.
1. Why did the French claim the whole Mississippi Valley as theirs?
2. Why was it a great crime for the Iroquois to kill almost the entire Huron tribe?
3. To whom did the land of Maine really belong?
4. Why did Father Marquette make another journey back to the Illinois Indians?
5. Why can you say that the French were sometimes unjust in trading with the Indians?

Our Lady

of

Knock

Pray for us

PRAYER

HAIL, most gracious Mother of Mercy hail, Mary, for whom we fondly yearn, through whom we obtain forgiveness, who would not love thee? Thou art our light in uncertainty, our comfort in sorrow, our solace in the time of trial, our refuge from every peril and temptation. Thou art our sure hope of salvation, second only to thy only-begotten Son; blessed are they who love thee, Our Lady! Incline, I beseech thee, thy ears of pity to the entreaties of this thy servant, a miserable sinner; dissipate the darkness of my sins by the bright beams of thy holiness, in order that I may be acceptable in thy sight.

(Indulgence of 500 days. S.P. Ap., April 22, 1941).

UNIT FOUR

HOMEMAKERS ALL

CHAPTER I—BEFORE THE MARCH BEGAN

Cabot explored the eastern coast of America for England.

Drake sailed around the world in 1577.

Sir Walter Raleigh's attempts to start a colony failed.

CHAPTER II—A PLANT MAKES A COLONY PAY

The first permanent English colony was established in Jamestown in 1607.

The first meeting of colonists who made their own laws in America took place in 1619.

Negro slaves entered Virginia in 1619.

CHAPTER III—LIBERTY IN THE CRADLE

Pilgrims came to Plymouth in 1620.

The Mayflower Compact gave the settlers self-government.

Town meetings were a pure form of democracy, but only Puritans could vote in the Massachusetts Bay colony.

Plymouth joined Massachusetts Bay Colon in 1691.

CHAPTER IV—ENGLISH CATHOLICS IN MARYLAND

Lord Baltimore tried to found a colony in Newfoundland.

Lord Baltimore founded Maryland in 1634.

The colonists setted at St. Mary's City in Maryland.

The Toleration Act of 1649 gave freedom of religion to Catholics and Protestants.

In 1689 Maryland Catholics were forbidden to practice their religion.

CHAPTER V —LET FREEDOM RING!

William Penn became a Quaker.

Pennsylvania was founded in 1682, for Quakers and other persecuted peoples.

William Penn and the Quakers settled in the city of Philadelphia.

William Penn made a famous treaty with the Indians which was never broken during his lifetime.

Penn made a set of laws for his colony, called the Great Law.

Penn's colony grew rapidly.

UNIT FOUR

HOMEMAKERS ALL

So FAR in your textbook, you have been reading about explorers and colonizers who were Catholics. The Spanish and French explorers spread the Catholic religion in America.

People of another country came to America in the early days. That country was England. England was once a great Catholic country.

About 1534, England started to break away from the Catholic Church. King Henry VIII refused to obey the Pope. Later, Queen Elizabeth started the English, or Anglican, Church.

Other religions sprang up in England. The English government persecuted Catholics as well as members of these new religions. Some people thought it best to leave England and make homes in America. There they could still live as Englishmen, with the right to worship God as they pleased.

People from England kept coming to America. Some came so that they could worship God as they thought best. Others came chiefly to earn a living in America.

All English colonists had one thing in common. They were all homemakers. Husbands brought their wives and children with them. They came to make America their home.

When the Spaniards came to America, they were too busy looking for gold to settle down. The French were quite satisfied to live at trading posts, where they could make a living by trading furs. But the English came to America because they were looking for freedom they had lost in England.

When the English came to America, they claimed the same rights they thought they should have had at home. Each colony had its own law-making body. No colony of France or Spain had this kind of freedom. The governor's word was the law they had to obey.

This unit tells about four colonies whose first settlers came directly from England in the seventeenth century. These colonies are Virginia, Massachusetts Bay, Maryland, and Pennsylvania.

The English people worked for freedom from very early times. In 1215, a great Catholic Archbishop, named Stephen Langton, helped to draw up a document called the Magna Carta. In English, these words mean "Great Charter."

The Great Charter set down a list of rights which even the king could not take away.

The ideas in the Great Charter are based on the teachings of the Catholic Church.

The English kings gave more and more freedom to the people they ruled. In 1295 the people of England were given a voice in making the laws.

CHAPTER I

BEFORE THE MARCH BEGAN

Looking Over the Chapter. Spain and France were not the only colonizers of the New World. England sent settlers in the early days.

A man named John Cabot explored for England in 1497. After this, nearly eighty years passed before another English ship sailed the high seas of the great Atlantic.

When Queen Elizabeth I ascended the throne of England, she decided to make England a rich and powerful nation. She knew that Spanish ships were bringing tons and tons of gold to Spain. She resolved that one day that gold would find a place in the treasury of England.

Elizabeth's daring sailors plundered and robbed Spanish colonies. Then they would sail home to England, proud of the store of riches they had with them. Can we praise the sailors for their daring deeds?

Spain was angry at England for this and other offenses. She attacked England in 1588. England was victorious, and Spain lost her great power on the seas. Her colonies suffered very much from this defeat.

Then England became mistress of the seas. It meant she could rule and rove wherever she wished on the ocean. This set the stage for the beginning of her colonies in the New World.

In this chapter you will read the story of England's first attempts to start a "little England" in the New World.

THE CABOTS MAKE A CLAIM

Cabot's Voyage. About the time of Columbus, an Italian boy joined the English navy. He was a very brave sailor, and was very anxious to find a northwest passage to India. He received the King's permission to try to find a waterway through the land that Columbus had discovered.

Columbus had three ships and one hundred thirty men for his journey. Cabot had only one small ship and eighteen men.

In 1497 Cabot sailed from a place in England called Bristol. He sailed directly across the Atlantic. He landed somewhere on the northeastern coast of America. He set up on the land the Cross of Saint George, and a standard bearing the name of England.

You know from the first unit of this text that Cabot was not the first man to visit the mainland of America. The Northmen, or Vikings, landed **208** here almost five hundred years before.

John Cabot found that the land was full of rocks. The nearby waters were full of fish. So plentiful were the fish that one had only to let a net down into the sea to make a fine catch. The fishing banks that Cabot discovered are known as the *Grand Banks of Newfoundland*. After this, the English made regular trips to the fishing banks of Newfoundland.

The English King thought very little of Cabot's trip. As a reward for his journey, he gave Cabot the sum of ten pounds (about fifty dollars), and then dismissed him. The King thought still less of Cabot's discovery the next year, when he heard that the Portuguese had found an ocean route to India.

Cabot, however, set out on another voyage with his son Sebastian.

Very little is known about these voyages of the Cabots. The little we do know was found in the letters of two Italians living in England at the time. These letters told very briefly about the voyages of their friends, the Cabots.

IN PRAISE OF PLUNDER

Ships and Money. Spain was the leading nation of Europe at the beginning of the sixteenth century. Her ships were the most powerful on the open seas. The gold of America made Spain a rich nation.

England felt that this wealth might be hers if

she would do something about it. She made up her mind to do something. She needed ships. She needed swift, small ships. Her ships must be as well fitted out as those of Spain. So England started building many ships during the time of Henry VIII.

Elizabeth's Plan. Elizabeth became queen in 1588. To make England a great nation, wealth was needed. To Elizabeth, the honor and glory of England was the greatest thing on earth. She did not care how she would make England wealthy. Honesty meant nothing to her. It only mattered that England should be the wealthy nation she planned.

England at last had a supply of ships of which Elizabeth was proud. These ships were smaller than Spain's vessels. They could travel faster, and could be quickly turned in any direction.

The English thought of a way by which enemy ships could be attacked near the water line. They planned to point heavy cannon through the holes on the sides of their ships. Many guns could be fired at once through these gun ports. The shot from these guns could damage and sink other ships. The English and the Spanish had many sea battles.

Moonlight Traders. The swift ships of England stole quietly and noiselessly into the ports of the Spanish settlements in America. There, in the moonlight, the English sold goods to the Spanish colonists. The English knew it was against the

Spanish law for Spanish colonists to trade with them.

In some places along the coast, the English "sea dogs" were kept from entering the ports by the Spanish governors. More often, the governor knew the English were at port but pretended not to know about it.

Men for Sale. In Central and South America, there was a great need for more people to work in the gold and silver mines.

The English saw this need when they came to trade with the colonists. The English soon went over to Africa. The Negro chiefs sold some of their own people to the English. They had no right to do this. The English also were guilty in purchasing human beings. Every human being is equal in the sight of God. It is wrong to sell anyone into slavery. It is also wrong to buy slaves.

The English chained these Negroes together, put them on the ships, and landed them at the Spanish ports. Here the Spaniards bought them from the English. Then these slaves had to work in the mines.

Pillage and Plunder. English sailors also landed in Spanish towns, often around the Isthmus of Panama. They would hide in some dark corner of the road. There they would lie in wait for the Spanish mule trains. These mule trains were carrying the gold from the mines to the ships in the harbor.

The English would rob and raid these mule trains. They knew they were stealing, but they did not care about that. They were gaining gold for England, the Queen, and themselves.

DRAKE, THE DRAGON

One of the most daring of England's sea dogs was the pirate, Francis Drake. When only eighteen, he owned a ship of his own. The King of Spain offered $200,000 to anyone who would capture him. Drake was so fierce an enemy of the Spanish that they nicknamed him "The Dragon."

In 1577, Drake was on one of his usual trips. He had a greater store of gold than ever before. He dared not sail home immediately, lest a Spanish vessel overtake him on the way. So he sailed along the eastern coast of South America.

Drake had only one of the five ships of his fleet left when he finally reached the Strait of Magellan. The remaining ship was the *Golden Hind*. He was now safe from the Spaniards. None of them had ever sailed through the Strait since Magellan discovered it. Drake was not afraid. He passed through the Strait and right into the Pacific.

Drake tried his luck at robbing Spanish ships. On one ship, bound for Panama, he captured twenty-six tons of silver, thirteen boxes of gold coins, and eighty pounds of gold. These Spaniards must have received a surprise to see an English ship on the Pacific Ocean.

Drake kept on sailing north until he reached the shores of California. There he landed, and claimed the land for England. Can you recall which nation finally settled California?

The Last Lap. Drake knew it would be more dangerous than ever to return to England by the same route. He determined to cross the Pacific and make a complete journey around the world. He sailed on and on. He knew that he was the second one ever to sail on these waters. When he reached England, he had several Spanish ships which he had captured, and a greater load of riches than ever before.

A Queenly Greeting. Queen Elizabeth was proud of her daring pirate. She hastened to his ship on his arrival. Touching him on the shoulder with a sword, she addressed him: "I dub thee knight, Sir Francis Drake." Do you think Sir Francis Drake should have received this honor? Had he done right in robbing, and stealing from others?

A GREAT SEA BATTLE

Spain decided to do something to stop England from robbing her colonies. She planned to crush England's growing navy. There were other reasons, also, why Spain and England were on unfriendly terms.

A large fleet of heavy Spanish vessels set out to defeat the English. Spain called her navy the "Great Armada" (ar-may'-day). The battle took place in the English Channel. Although the Spaniards fought well, the light English ships moved very rapidly. This gave England a great advantage over the Spanish. There were Catholics in the English navy who fought along with their Protestant countrymen to defend their country. The faith was not yet dead in England, though Elizabeth had tried her best to make it so.

A storm arose, in which many Spanish ships were wrecked, and only a few reached home. The rest of the Spanish fleet sailed north around Scotland, and back home again to Spain.

Spain lost, the English won. All this took place in the year 1588.

The defeat of the Spanish Armada was the

turning point of the tide for England. From that day on, Spain began to lose her power in America. England had the power to rule the seas, afraid of no rival nation. Very soon, the English would come to America. The path was cleared for England's great march of colonizers to America.

A POOR BEGINNING

While Elizabeth was still Queen of England, a very handsome young man, Sir Walter Raleigh (raw'-lee), lived at the palace. He had been in many wars and had been on expeditions to the New World. He was more of a poet and writer than explorer.

A story is told that one day when the Queen

was walking near her palace she came upon a puddle of mud. This young man stepped forward, took off his fine velvet cloak, and placed it over the puddle. Elizabeth was pleased by this act and gave Raleigh many honors.

Raleigh told Queen Elizabeth that if she wanted to become rich from the lands of America, she must send people over there to live.

Trying to Get Started. The Queen thought Raleigh's plan was a good one. Then she remembered the trip that John Cabot had made eighty-eight years before. She said that the land along the coast of North America rightfully belonged to England. She decided, therefore, that England should settle on some of these lands.

The Spanish had founded the city of St. Augustine in 1565. Many years before, the French explored farther north. The English were not to be left out of this great race for lands and fortunes in the New World. The Queen told Sir Walter Raleigh he could have all the land he wanted on which to start a colony.

More than lands were needed to start a colony. Sir Walter Raleigh had to supply everything else that was needed. Finally, in the summer of 1585, all was ready. This was only a few years before the defeat of the Spanish Armada.

The Queen would not allow Sir Walter Raleigh to leave England. However, the colony was supported by his money. The little group of colonists landed on Roanoke Island off the coast of what is now North Carolina, near the Virginia border. They remained there during the winter.

Queen Elizabeth was so pleased with the reports that she named the land Virginia in her honor. She liked to be called "The Virgin Queen." The land of Virginia included the whole Atlantic coast north of Florida.

At first the Indians were friendly, but after a while, the colonists disagreed with them. Just at this time, Sir Francis Drake was sailing by. He stopped to see how the colonists were getting along. The colonists were so unhappy that they all boarded his ship and returned with him to England. You can imagine how surprised the people in England were to see them.

Potatoes and Tobacco. This first English colony in America failed. However, it had one important result. The colonists took back to England some potatoes and some tobacco plants.

The people of England had never seen the tobacco plant before. It soon became very popular in England for men to use tobacco.

The potatoes were planted in Ireland on land owned by Sir Walter Raleigh. They grew very, very well on this land. Ever since, they have been one of the chief crops of Ireland.

Lost Forever. Two years later, another band of colonists came to Roanoke Island, with John White as governor.

On landing at Roanoke Island, the new colonists found the log cabins that had been built by the colonists before them.

John White was the grandfather of a baby girl, named Virginia Dare. Virginia was the first child to be born of English parents in the land now called the United States.

After some time, the supplies were nearly all gone. John White, very unwillingly, went back to England to get more supplies from Sir Walter Raleigh.

Governor White was very sad, for he had to leave his daughter and little Virginia Dare.

This was in 1588, the year of the Spanish Armada. White had to fight in this great sea battle.

Two years had passed before he could return to Virginia.

When he returned, he found no one on Roanoke Island. But he did find the word "Croatan" carved on the bark of a tree. This was the name of an island not far away. John White went to this island but found no one. No one knows what became of the colonists. They may have starved to death, or may have been killed by the Indians or the Spaniards.

England's Debt to Raleigh. Sir Walter Raleigh's first colonists returned. His second colony disappeared. He now had nothing to show for the large sums of money he had spent.

However, Sir Walter Raleigh is called the "Father of English Colonization." He is called this because he taught England the value of colonies in America. He once said that Virginia would yet become a great nation. We shall see later if his words came true.

Later, Sir Walter Raleigh was put to death by the English government. Although he had done a great deal to help found colonies in the New World, his work was not appreciated.

Very often the work that men do is not appreciated. The government for whom they work does not reward them.

We should learn from this fact that it is better to work for God and do His holy will than to work only for money and riches.

God always rewards us for the things we do for Him. Men often forget others and are even cruel to them.

The way to learn to work for God and to do His will is to follow the teachings of the Catholic Church.

Are These Words Your Own?

Croatan	gracious	offenses	evil
Armada	plunder	rival	

Lest We Forget

1. Start making a time-line of English explorers and colonizers.
2. Show on another time-line the chief explorations in America from 1492 to 1600. Place the colonizers of France and Spain on this time-line also. The outlines at the beginning of each unit will help you remember the important dates.

Have You Mastered This Chapter?

If you can answer these questions, you have studied this chapter well.

1. Name England's first explorer of American lands.
2. In what part of America did slavery exist in 1500?
3. Compare the voyages of Cabot and Verrazano.
4. Compare the routes of Magellan and Drake around the world.
5. Show why slavery in Central and South America was a great evil.
6. How did the Spanish Armada turn the eyes of England towards America?
7. Show why England's sailors should not have been rewarded by Elizabeth on their return from America.
8. Why is Raleigh's name connected with tobacco today?

CHAPTER II

A PLANT MAKES A COLONY PAY

Looking Over the Chapter. At the end of the sixteenth century, two English colonies were started in America. Both of these failed. Shortly after this, England gained full control of the seas. Her ships were now free to sail wherever they chose.

In a few years, a new colony was founded. In the beginning, the settlers feared starvation. They feared, too, the spears and arrows of the Indians. It looked as if this colony, also, was going to fail.

Instead, this colony grew to be England's first permanent colony. This did not happen because the colonists found gold or silver, or because they found precious wood in the American forests. No, it was a plant that made it possible for Virginia to send riches to England. That plant was tobacco.

Virginia was not only the first English colony to succeed in America, but it brought to the New World a new kind of freedom. England allowed the colonists to take part in making their laws. The **221**

Spanish and French colonists were not allowed to do this. In a later textbook of this series, we shall see that Americans today take part in making their laws.

ENGLAND'S FIRST COLONY

The London Company Is Formed. After Elizabeth's death, many Englishmen became interested in colonies in the New World. In London, a group of merchants and businessmen decided to form a *company*. Its purpose was to furnish what was needed to start a colony. Each man was to pay a certain amount of the expenses. Each one was promised a share in the profits of the colony if it made good.

This group of men was called the London Company. King James gave them permission to start a colony. They promised him a share in the profits. They were told that they might start a colony on land in Virginia.

The members of the London Company did not come to America. Instead, they sent about one hundred men who were willing to make their homes in America. These men were promised the same privileges as citizens who lived in England. These and other rights were written down when the London Company received the permission or charter to start a colony.

A Colony in Virginia. It was 1607 when the three ships started out carrying the brave band of Englishmen. A man named Newport was captain of the group. Captain Newport had a letter which he was not allowed to open until the ships reached the New World. This letter contained the names of those who were to govern the colony, and the kind of work the colonists were to do when they arrived. There were no Catholics among these colonists. England was no longer a Catholic country. The King of England had disobeyed the Pope and, in 1534, had broken away from the Catholic Church. Later, Queen Elizabeth started a church of her own and called it the Church of England. The English government was very cruel to Catholics who would not give up their faith and join the new church.

The journey was made by way of the Canary Islands to the West Indies, and then up along the coastline from the south. The colonists were four long months at sea before reaching Virginia.

The colonists came to a large river. They sailed up this river to a spot which was surrounded on three sides by water. Here they landed. They called the settlement Jamestown in honor of their King.

The very day the colonists arrived, they were attacked by a band of Indians, and some were wounded and one killed. Later the colonists built a large fort, and around this fort they built a high fence called a stockade.

When Captain Newport went back to England, **223**

he took a load of timber with him. This was just what the London Company wanted. England needed more and more wood each year to build ships, and there were few forests in England. The merchants were happy when they heard of the forests of tall trees in the New World.

Jamestown, the land where the colonists settled, was low and marshy. No fresh-water springs were found there. When the heat of the first summer came, the mosquitoes were so bad that many of the colonists died from malaria. The colonists could easily have chosen a better place for settlement.

Making Lazy People Work. This unhealthy place was not the cause of all the trouble. Some of the colonists did not want to work. They preferred to hunt for gold. When the food supply gave out, they had to hunt or fish. Many of the colonists were not used to hunting and fishing, and they were afraid to leave the settlement because of the Indians.

The colonists became sick and hungry. They also became homesick. By autumn, only about fifty men were left in the colony.

The colonists selected one of these men as their leader. He was John Smith, a brave soldier. When Smith took command of the colony he made a rule which said: "If you do not work, you shall not eat." This rule was necessary because some of the colonists' troubles were due to laziness.

Then John Smith decided to lay in a food supply. He was sure he could get meat and corn from the Indians.

Saved by an Indian Maid. One day when John Smith and two companions were on an exploring trip through the woods, they met a band of Indians. The Indians killed one of the men, and the other escaped. Captain John Smith was taken captive. The Indians took him to their warlike chief, Powhatan (pow-ha-tan'). The chief said John Smith must die. The story is told that just as an Indian was going to beat John Smith to death with a war club, a young Indian girl rushed up to him. She threw herself between the Indian and Captain Smith. This girl was the chief's daughter, Pocahontas (poke-a-hon'-tas). She begged her father to spare Captain Smith's life.

Powhatan could not refuse the request of his beautiful daughter, and he saved John Smith's life. Powhatan became a friend of John Smith and the colonists. He helped them in many ways until he died in 1618.

Later Pocahontas married a colonist named John Rolfe. She went to England with him, but found the English ways of living very strange. When Pocahontas and her husband were preparing to return to Virginia, she became ill and died in England among strangers. You can imagine how lonely Pocahontas must have been.

For two years Captain Smith worked hard as a leader of the little colony. In 1609, more colon- **225** ists arrived, increasing the number of settlers to five hundred. Unfortunately, John Smith was wounded in a gunpowder explosion. He was burned so badly that he had to return to England.

Bad Times Come Again. Without their leader, Captain John Smith, some of the colonists soon returned to their lazy habits and refused to work.

Besides this, seven more shiploads of colonists arrived from England.

In the winter of 1609, there was not enough food in the storehouse for all these people. Many starved to death. Others died of diseases. The severe cold of the winter months caused the death of many. The colonists had good reason for calling this period the "Starving Time." If only they had

had another leader like Captain John Smith, something might have been done.

Saved by a Ship. At the end of the winter, only sixty colonists were still alive. They decided to return to England. They crowded into two small ships and started for England. It looked as if this would be the end of the colony.

Just as the colonists reached the mouth of the James River, they saw an English ship coming towards them. To their great joy, the ship contained not only supplies, but also a leader for the colony. He was Lord Delaware. In the beginning, Captain Smith saved the colony from failure. Now an English ship saved the colonists from giving up Jamestown.

Lord Delaware was a good leader. He built two forts for the colonists. He divided the work so that each man was given certain duties to perform. However, after a short time, he became ill and had to leave the colony.

A Stern Ruler. Sir Thomas Dale was the next man to govern the colony. He gave each man three acres of land to work upon in raising crops. Each colonist was allowed to keep all he produced except six bushels of corn. This went into the public storehouse. Now much more food was grown than ever before.

Dale also had all the laws of the colony written down. He governed the colony well, but was very severe.

A Plant Pays Profits. The colony was not making England rich. There was no gold here to make the English King happy. In the beginning, Sir Thomas Dale would not allow the colonists to raise tobacco. He thought it was a useless crop. Besides, the tobacco raised by the Indians in Virginia was not so pleasing as that from the West Indies. Do you remember where Columbus first saw people smoking the leaves of the tobacco plant?

Among the group of colonists who arrived from England in 1609, there was a young man named John Rolfe. He knew that the English liked tobacco. Rolfe was a good farmer. Therefore, he decided to try planting some tobacco. By 1612, he produced tobacco "as sweet, strong, and pleasant" as that grown elsewhere.

Up to this time the colonists had raised only corn, but soon after Rolfe's experiment, tobacco became the chief product. This was after Governor Dale had gone back to England. Fifteen years later, half a million pounds of Virginia tobacco were sold in London. Tobacco made the colonists rich. It gave rich profits to the London Company, too. People began to pay their bills in pounds of tobacco, because tobacco was as valuable as money. No wonder, then, that we speak of tobacco as the gold of the Virginia colony.

The colonists were very glad when Governor **228** Dale was called back to England. Sir Samuel

Argall was appointed in his place. But the colonists did not fare much better under him. He was cruel and dishonest. He preferred to make money for himself rather than to make the colony a sound success.

While Argall was governor, he traveled to Maine, where he destroyed a Jesuit mission. He went as far north as Acadia, where he destroyed the French settlement.

PEOPLE BECOME LAWMAKERS

WHEN the men in the London Company heard of the cruel, selfish, and dishonorable actions of Governor Argall, they went to the King. They told him that they wanted the governor to have less power and the people of the colony to have more.

The King appointed a new governor and gave him permission to give more power to the people. Governor Argall returned to England in disgrace.

Beginning of Freedom. Governor Yeardley was the new governor. The first thing he did was to call a meeting in Jamestown. At this time there were eleven settlements in Virginia. In each of these settlements, two men were elected by the colonists to go to this meeting.

The men who were going to speak for the colonists were called *burgesses*. This name was used in England for men who represented the people in Parliament.

The twenty-two burgesses met in a little log **229**

church in Jamestown in 1619. The governor was also present. The meeting opened with a prayer. After that the burgesses took an oath of loyalty to the King. Then they voted to approve the seal, or sign of the colony. Seals were used to stamp important papers. The burgesses decided that they would act on all tax laws. They held the meeting in the same way as they would have done if they had been still living in England. This was a great moment in our history.

August 4, 1619, was the first time that people in any part of the Western Hemisphere were allowed to vote in the making of their laws.

This was a very important act in the history of America. It was the beginning of one kind of freedom we enjoy in the New World. We have many other kinds of freedom.

The Spanish colonists had freely agreed to many of the good laws that had come to them from their kings in Spain. The English colonists chose to make their own laws in the New World. Long before that, in England, the people had fought for and obtained the right to have a voice in the making of laws.

The English colonists carried that freedom to America.

As long as Virginia was a colony, the House of Burgesses continued to meet. They talked things over with the governor, and passed laws
for the good of the colony. As the years passed,

other English colonists settled along the coast.
They copied this kind of government.

OTHER EVENTS OF THE GREAT YEAR

Huts Become Homes. This was not the only important event of 1619, the "Great Year," as it is

called. Two other very important events took place.

In 1619 there were only a few women among the colonists. In that year, the London Company sent over ninety women to become wives of the English planters. Now the Virginia planters could raise families and start homes. Now they could work, and pray, and play around their own fireplaces.

Making Slaves of Equals. We have seen that tobacco very quickly became the chief means of support in the colonies. The planters increased the size of their farms in order to raise more and more tobacco. More tobacco meant more money for them. In order to raise more tobacco, the planters had to have more laborers in their fields. They found it was very hard to get laborers, for very few men wanted to spend the long hot days in the tobacco fields.

In 1619 a Dutch ship brought twenty Negroes to Jamestown. Here the captain sold them to Virginia planters. The planters owned these Negroes just as they might own an animal. They made them work in the tobacco fields just as if they were animals. These Virginians committed a great wrong. They made slaves of people who were equal to them in the sight of God, their loving Father, Who has created all of us.

That is how slavery entered the land that is now the United States. Here is where it began. You will learn more about slavery in the textbook, *Challenge of Freedom.*

Workers from England. A planter's land was called a plantation. The planters found another way to get workers. There were in England some poor white people who wanted to work in America. The planters would pay the fare for these poor people to cross the ocean if they would work as

232 servants for about three years.

The planter and servant would sign papers stating that both agreed to these terms. This paper was called an *indenture,* because it had a dotted line in the middle of the paper. The paper could be torn easily on the dotted line. The servant was called an *indentured servant.* You will read more about these indentured servants.

Servants Become Planters. It was no disgrace for white people to be indentured servants. They freely made the promise to work for another for a certain time. When this time was up, they were free to work for pay. Then they would buy their own land. Some of them became wealthy and hired indentured servants for themselves.

This way of hiring indentured servants continued for a long time. It continued even after Virginia became a state.

LIFE ON A PLANTATION

A World in Itself. On the broad land of the plantations, some of the colonists built beautiful houses. The plantations were little villages in themselves. When the planter needed some new clothes or a pair of shoes, he did not go to town or to the city as we do today. There were shops on his plantation where such things were made or sold. Customers paid pounds of tobacco for what they needed.

The plantation owner led a very busy life. However, he took time for fox-hunting with his hounds **233** during the day. He often danced or played cards with friends during the winter evenings.

School Life of the Colonists' Children. Because the plantations were so far apart, no schools were built. Men or women were hired to teach the children in the planters' homes. These teachers were called tutors. The older boys were usually sent to college in England.

Town Life in Virginia. The town people were mostly traders and storekeepers. These people were poorer than the plantation owners. There were no schools in the towns. The only education the children received was what their parents gave them.

However, there were churches. Everyone had

to go to church on Sunday. In 1610 a law was passed concerning attendance at church. These were the punishments for failing to go to church: "The first time, a fine; for the second, a whipping; and for the third, to suffer death."

Thirteen years later the second and third punishments were taken away, but the heavy fine remained. You must remember that this church was not the Catholic Church. It was the Church of England.

THE KING CLAIMS THE COLONY

In 1622, an Indian attack was made on Jamestown in which many, many colonists lost their lives. Plantation houses and settlements were burned.

When King James heard about this, he became alarmed. He was afraid that the London Company had not protected the settlers properly. Other reports against the London Company also displeased him. He decided to take over the colony for himself. From that time on, the governor was appointed by the King. The colony was then called a "crown colony," or a "royal colony."

The colonists asked, however, that they might continue to have a voice in the government through the meetings of the House of Burgesses. This request was granted.

Coming of the Cavaliers. About this time there was a change of government in England. The King **235**

was killed, and the government was taken over by Parliament. Anyone who was true to the King was not safe in England. Those who were true to the King were called Cavaliers.

Among the Cavaliers who came to Virginia at this time was the Washington family. They bought a large plantation here and gave their children a fine education.

WHEN RICHES RULED

In 1660, England had a King again. He sent Sir William Berkeley to Virginia as governor. Berkeley was a stubborn and selfish man. He made friends of the wealthy planters. He did not make them pay their taxes, while the poorer planters had to pay heavy taxes.

At this time the members of the House of Burgesses were mostly rich planters. This happened because Berkeley had not had an election of new members for sixteen years. The poorer families of Virginia had no part in the making of the laws, because Berkeley wanted his wealthy friends to sit in the House of Burgesses.

The poor colonists were in great danger from the Indians, too. Often lonely settlers were found dead among their burned cabins.

Governor Berkeley knew about these wrongs. He did nothing to stop the Indians, because he was making a large fortune for himself by trading furs with them.

The People Rebel. A rich young planter named Bacon decided to do something about the way the poor colonists were being treated. He raised a little army and met the Indians in war. He killed many of them in a fierce battle.

Berkeley was angry and called Bacon a rebel. He tried to capture Bacon but failed. Then the governor ran away from Jamestown.

Bacon burned the Jamestown settlement and then went back to his plantation. He died one month later.

But Berkeley was still angry. When he came back to the colony, he sent for all those who had fought with Bacon. He promised to forgive them. When they came to him he had them hanged as rebels. That was his kind of revenge.

King Charles II was very angry about these murders. When this wicked governor returned to England, King Charles refused to see him and he died in disgrace.

Bacon's rebellion showed that the colonists were willing to fight for freedom from unjust rulers. It showed that they demanded just taxation, and that both rich and poor be treated fairly. That is why Bacon's Rebellion is one of the first steps towards the freedom we enjoy today.

Williamsburg, the Capital. The second college in the colonies was opened in 1693. Now the sons of rich planters could go to college in America. This college was built at Williamsburg, Virginia. It was called the College of William and Mary in honor of the new King and Queen of England. Do you recall the date when the first college in the colonies was opened?

In 1699, the capital of the Virginia colony was moved to Williamsburg. It was a very gay and fashionable town then. It remained the capital of

Virginia until the American colonies gained their independence in 1783.

Williamsburg Today. In 1927, some wealthy men gave large sums of money to have the town of Williamsburg rebuilt. Today it looks almost the same as it did in colonial times.

Many women in Williamsburg sometimes dress in colonial style, just as the Virginians did. The **238** men sometimes walk on the streets of Williamsburg in the same kind of clothes that George Washington wore in his day. The people of Williamsburg do this in order to help Americans to have some idea of their own colonial history. Many thousands of people visit this town each year. On page 238 there is a picture of one of the buildings in Williamsburg.

It would be a good idea to visit Williamsburg sometime. It is a very beautiful town, and it gives visitors a very good idea of what life was like in colonial times.

It is a good thing to see all these things, because then we will be able to understand better the lessons taught in our history books.

We should always try to know as much about our country as we can. A good way to do this is to go to places in your own town or city that date back to olden times. Get to know these places so you can obtain some idea of what life was like in the past. This will make you feel closer to the people who have gone before us and have made this country great.

New Words to Conquer

burgess	rebellion	approve
plantation	colonial	seal
Parliament	Cavalier	tutor
profits	stockade	representatives
indentured	product	

Can You Work by Yourself?

If you can do any of the following activities by

yourself, your teacher will know that you are a good student.

1. Place the important dates of this chapter on your time-line, which you began in Chapter I.

2. On an outline map of North America, fill in the places where the first Spanish colony settled. Do the same for the first French and English colonies.

3. Prepare a paragraph of four or five sentences, telling the story of any one of the following:
   a. Tobacco in Virginia
   b. Slavery in Virginia
   c. Freedom in Virginia
   d. Bacon's Rebellion
   e. John Smith's Life
   f. Plantation Life in Virginia

Points to Think About and Discuss

1. Why were Negroes brought to Virginia? Tell why it was wrong to buy and sell Negroes.

2. In what ways were indentured servants better off than Negroes?

3. Prove that Captain John Smith was a good leader.

4. Explain how a soldier and a ship saved the Virginia colony at different times.

5. Does the United States today have a body of men who make laws as the House of Burgesses did? Where do they meet?

6. Explain: "Virginia's gold was tobacco."

7. Prove that 1619 was a *Great Year*.

8. Tell how a boy on a plantation lived differently from a boy who lived in one of the towns.

9. What do you think is the most important act in the history of the Virginia colony? Why?

10. Why was it wrong for Berkeley to kill the men who took part in Bacon's Rebellion?

CHAPTER III

LIBERTY IN THE CRADLE

THE COLONY of Virginia was founded in 1607. A little while afterwards, another group of Englishmen came to build homes in the land of freedom. Their settlement was quite far away from the tobacco fields of Virginia. These settlers were called Pilgrims.

The Pilgrims ruled themselves and appointed their own governors. Freedom such as this was never enjoyed in Virginia.

Ten years later, another group of people came to the northeast coast of America. They settled on the shores of Massachusetts Bay at a place called Boston. They built homes and churches. These people were known as Puritans, and only Puritan people could enjoy complete freedom in the Massachusetts Bay Colony.

These people were allowed to pass their own laws and appoint their own governor. They decided how much taxes they would pay, whether or not they should build a school with their funds, or build a new road in the settlement. All these things were talked over at their town meetings.

Everyone could go to these meetings. However, when it came time to vote, only the Puritan people could take part.

The colonists of Massachusetts Bay enjoyed their freedom. This love of freedom grew stronger as the years went on. It continued to grow until one day a new nation was born.

In this chapter you will study about the early days in the Plymouth Colony and the Massachusetts Bay Colony when the Pilgrims and Puritans arrived. We say that those were the days of "Liberty in the Cradle."

RELIGIOUS TROUBLES IN ENGLAND

FOR MANY hundreds of years, England had been a Catholic country. The English people loved Our Lady so much, the country was called "Mary's Dower." This meant the country belonged to Our Blessed Lady.

But England did not remain a Catholic country. In the sixteenth century, a great change began to take place. The king of England at that time was Henry VIII. He started a movement away from Christ's true Church. This ended in separating many people from the Catholic Church. The new church that started in England was a Protestant Church, known as the Church of England.

Separatists. Some of the people who joined the new Church of England soon grew to dislike their new religion. They did not like this new Church any better than they liked the Catholic Church. They started to separate themselves from the Church of England. Because of this, they are called *Separatists*.

These people refused to go to the King's church or to support it. Instead, they assembled every Sunday in meeting places of their own.

One of these groups of Separatists lived in the small village of Scrooby, England. Their meeting place was the home of a very popular schoolmaster of the village, William Brewster. One of the Separatists who attended the meetings was a young man named William Bradford.

Bound for Holland. The King of England, James I, was very angry with these Separatists. He punished them for refusing to attend the Church of England. The Separatists thought it better to leave England and settle in some other land. They made secret plans to go to Holland, where they would be allowed to attend their own church on Sunday. Can you find Holland on your map?

The Separatists crossed the English Channel, and went to Holland. It was in the City of Amsterdam that they first made their homes. They did not stay there, because the people of the city did not have much love for any religion. Then the Separatists went to live farther south, in the city of Leyden (lie'-den).

In Leyden the Separatists found life very **243**

much different from that in England. Most of them worked in weaving factories. This was much harder for them than hoeing and planting their farms in England.

Although these people had warm and comfortable homes in Leyden, still they were unhappy. Their children spoke Dutch all the time, went to Dutch schools, and played with Dutch boys and girls. They wanted their children to learn to speak English well, and to grow up as real English people.

Other things made the Separatists unhappy. War was going on in Europe, and times were getting harder. Soon there would be no work for them at all. Where could they go?

Leaving Holland. Many of them had read about Captain John Smith and the Virginia colony. To start a colony in America seemed the only thing they could do.

Thoughts of a long trip to America made the Separatists afraid. They knew they would have to face many hardships when they arrived. But these things did not keep them from going.

The Separatists were poor people. They could not pay for their trip to America. A rich man in London named Thomas Weston offered to help them. In return for helping them, the Separatists were to put everything they earned into a storehouse and use only what was necessary. Then at the end of seven years, half of what was in the

storehouse belonged to Weston's company. The

other half could be divided among the Separatists. These were hard terms, but the Separatists agreed to them.

The Departure. Thirty-five of the little group in Holland left for Plymouth in England. Among them was Miles Standish, a very well trained soldier, but not a Separatist. He was the only member of the colony who did not become a member of this religion. Two ships, the *Mayflower* and the *Speedwell* set sail for America. Not far out, the *Speedwell* began to leak, and both ships had to return to England. On September 16, 1620, the *Mayflower* again started out from Plymouth. This time there were a hundred and two people crowded on board. These people were traveling to a land far from their home. We call such travelers *pilgrims*. That is why these Separatists are often called "The Pilgrims." Hereafter, we shall refer to the Separatists as Pilgrims.

The trip across was very stormy. More than once they were in danger of sinking. The journey was finished after sixty-five days. Now an ocean liner makes the same trip in four or five days, and an airplane can cross in several hours.

ON NEW ENGLAND SHORES

At Cape Cod. In November, 1620, the *Mayflower* was driven by storms on to a stony coast at the tip of Cape Cod. This was the land Captain Smith had called New England. This was much farther **245**

north than the land on which they had permission to settle. But the *Mayflower* could go no farther.

As soon as they landed, the women got busy washing clothes on the edge of the river. The men looked around to see what kind of land it was. They returned before dark, and decided to call the land their home.

A Great Document. Even before they left the boat, they had begun to plan what kind of government they wanted. The men got together and made a written agreement, or compact. They agreed to make just laws which would be for the good of the colony. They agreed to elect one of the group to be their governor. Because this agreement was made on board the *Mayflower,* it was called the **246** *Mayflower Compact.*

This was something never heard of before. A colony in the New World had decided to appoint its own governors, and make its own laws. This colony ruled itself for seventy years afterwards.

The Separatists governed their own colony from the very beginning. They had more self-government than the Virginia colony. It was only

right that they should govern themselves. God created all men free and equal, so all men should have some say in governing themselves. The Separatists appointed John Carver, who had been with them in Holland, to be their first governor.

Settling Down. It took them many days to find a good place to settle. When they found it, they called it Plymouth. Do you know why? **247**

There is a story that when they landed, some of them used a large rock on the shore as a stepping-stone. Then, it is said, they knelt down to thank God for their safe arrival. This rock has been carefully preserved in memory of the landing of the Pilgrims. It has been on the beach, in Pilgrim Hall in Plymouth, and in the town square. Now it is safe behind an iron railing.

The winter was a very bad time for these poor people to try to build homes. The ground was frozen, and there was nothing but stony land and forest around them. They suffered much during that first winter. Bitter cold and poor food brought sickness to many. Forty of them died that winter.

The colonists tried to hide the graves they dug, so that the Indians would not know how few were left to defend the little colony. At one time, only six or seven colonists were well enough to take care of the others.

Governor Carver died at this time. William Bradford was elected to take his place. He governed the colony so well that he was kept as governor for thirty-one years.

Indians Become Friends. One day in March, the little group of Pilgrims was surprised to see a friendly Indian come up to them, and say in English, "Welcome, Englishmen!" This Indian's name was Samoset (sam'-o-set). He had learned a little English from the fishermen who stopped along the coast to dry their fish. Samoset left, but returned a little later with another Indian named Squanto (skwan'-toe). Squanto had been kidnapped and taken to England, where he had learned to speak English well. A kind-hearted man in England heard that he had been kidnapped and sent him back to his own people. Squanto was forever grateful to the Puritans.

SPRINGTIME IN PLYMOUTH

The Pilgrims were very fortunate to have such good friends as Samoset and Squanto. Squanto taught them the best way to plant their crops in New England soil. He taught them, too, where they could get the best catch of fish.

A Treaty with the Indians. Squanto's chief, Massasoit (mass'-a-soit), wanted to come to visit the New England settlement. The Pilgrims formed a parade and went out to meet the kind chief. Massasoit promised to live in peace with the Pilgrims. The Pilgrims then made the first New England treaty with the Indians. For fifty years, the Indians and the Pilgrims kept their promises to live in peace. This shows how people of different races can live together in peace.

Unfriendly Indians. Canonicus (can-on'-i-cus) was the head of a group of unfriendly Indians. One day he sent to Governor Bradford a bundle of long, sharp arrows wrapped up in a snakeskin. Can you guess the meaning of this message?

Governor Bradford talked with Miles Standish, **249**

the military leader, to see what should be done. They planned to show the Indians that they were not afraid of them. They filled the snakeskin with gunpowder and shot, in place of the arrows, and sent it back to Canonicus.

The Indian Chief did not expect anything like this. Canonicus quickly ordered the snakeskin to

be taken away. He did not send any further messages to the Pilgrims.

THE FIRST NEW ENGLAND HOMES

The colonists had a very busy time in Plymouth. More cabins were needed. A sawmill was **250** built to cut logs to build the cabins. Most of these cabins had only one large room. This room was used as a living room, kitchen, workshop and bedroom. Often the stables and sheds for the animals were joined to the cabin so that they could be easily reached in bad winter weather.

The principal part of the cabin was the open fireplace. Around this fireplace all meals were prepared, work was done, games were played, and lessons were studied. The Pilgrims spent many happy hours around the cheerful fireplaces of home.

In another corner of the one-room cabin stood the spinning wheel. On this, the Pilgrim women spun flax for thread, and wool for yarn. Near the spinning wheel stood the loom, where the thread was woven into cloth called "homespun."

At night the only light in the cabins was the light from candles or from the fireplace. During the day, a little light came in through the high, small, framed windows. Oiled paper was placed in these windows to keep out the rain and wind.

The chairs were made of logs covered with fur. There were a few beds, but most people slept on the floor.

In the summer of the first year in Plymouth a new building was put up which was used as a church and a fort. It was called the "meeting-house." In it were some rough benches, and a place for the minister. There was no altar in this meeting-house. Do you know why?

Sunday in Plymouth. Every Sunday morning a drum was sounded, and the Pilgrims gathered in front of the home of Miles Standish. All the men, women, and children walked reverently in procession to the meeting-house. They were dressed in quaint simple clothes. They were led by the governor and the pastor. All the men carried their guns. Can you guess why?

The service lasted all day, with only a little rest for lunch. If a lady fell asleep, the usher would go to her and tickle her nose with a feather fastened to one end of a long rod. If a man feel asleep, the usher would go the sleeping man and tap his head with the rabbit's foot fastened to the other end of the rod.

THANKFUL PEOPLE

The Pilgrims had been in Plymouth for almost a year. Eleven houses had been built, four of them big enough for a large group of people to live in. Their fields were well cared for. From them they gathered a harvest of corn, wheat, peas, beans, barley, and oats. There was enough corn to double their weekly ration.

They also had a good supply of fish. This fish was well salted to keep it fresh for the winter months. Wild geese, turkeys, and other animals were plentiful. The Pilgrims were very happy because they were at peace with the Indians, and **252** there had been no disease lately.

A Christian Thanksgiving. The Pilgrims had stored up goods for the long winter ahead. They had many things for which to be thankful. So, in 1621, Governor Bradford ordered the Pilgrims to set aside a few days for a celebration in thanksgiving to God for His goodness to them.

The Pilgrims invited the Indians to the party. The Indians accepted the invitation and brought presents of wild turkeys and deer meat.

First, there was a short entertainment. The small army of Miles Standish put on a show of fine drills and formations. The audience was very pleased with the performance of the soldiers.

Then came time for dinner. The red-skinned Indians and "pale-faced" Pilgrims sat side-by-side around a large table. The Pilgrims knew that the color of their own skin did not put them on a higher level than the Indians. The Pilgrims knew that all men are children of the same Father in heaven. Were they right about this? How can we show we believe all men are brothers?

The great feast lasted three days. There was plenty of food for all. Among their dishes were turkey, fruit, all kinds of cooked vegetables, succotash, cranberries, corn cake, and several kinds of pies. Every year afterwards, the Pilgrims kept up the celebration. The custom spread to other New England colonies and later to colonies south of New England.

We still celebrate Thanksgiving Day. It is cele- **253**

brated each year on the fourth Thursday of November. This custom has continued for many years in our country.

IN PEACEFUL PLYMOUTH

Living like Freemen. In the beginning of Plymouth Colony, all food that was grown was loaded in a common storehouse, except for the amount

needed to live on. But in 1623, Governor Bradford divided the land, giving each settler about three acres as his own. After that, farmers could keep everything grown on their own farms, except for the amount which they gave for the common storehouse.

Now each farmer worked harder than ever. He

wanted to be proud of his own little farm. Fences of stone were built around the farms. This stone was gathered from the New England hillsides.

Colonists Buy Their Colony. Nearly seven years had passed since the Pilgrims came to America. It was now time for them to keep their promise to Thomas Weston's Company.

The colonists got together and talked things over. They were honest people and knew they had a debt to pay. They thought of another way of paying their honest debts. It was a fair way, too.

They agreed to pay back the money loaned them when they left Holland, rather than give up the products of their labors. They had to borrow money from England at this time in order to do this. Weston's Company accepted the money in place of the goods. Now the Pilgrims owned the colony themselves. This freedom to own land was a new thing in America.

The Pilgrims ruled themselves from the very beginning. But to them freedom was something for themselves alone. No one had any rights in the colony except members of the Separatist religion. This was a very selfish way of living.

An Important Colony. Plymouth Colony was important because of the kind of freedom it gave to its colonists. In Virginia, the colonists made their own laws, but these laws had to be approved by the governor, who was appointed by the King.

In Plymouth the people appointed their own **255**

governor, and their rules became law without anyone else's approval. After a while this freedom was taken away from the Pilgrims. But the people of New England were so used to this freedom that they were not happy until they got it back again in 1776. This was the time of the signing of the Declaration of Independence.

A THRONGED COLONY

Protestants Splitting Up. While the Pilgrims were plowing the land on their New England farms, more trouble lay ahead in England. The King of England, Charles I, was having a hard time trying to make the people support the Church of England.

Another group of Englishmen broke away from the Church of England. These people complained that the King's church was too much like the Catholic Church. They wanted to "purify" or "clean up" the Church of England by doing away with everything that was like the Catholic Church. Because they wanted to "purify" the Church of England they were called *Puritans*.

The Catholics had statues and music in their churches. They celebrated feast days. The Puritans wanted none of these things in their churches. They did not even want Christmas, and Christmas had always been a great day of holy rejoicing in England. Christmas means "Christ's Mass." The

Puritans changed that name to "Christ-tide" because they had no respect or love for the Holy Sacrifice of the Mass.

The Puritans had very severe ideas. They thought Sunday so sacred that they would not take a walk, play a game, or even cook a meal on that day. The Puritans could not live happily in England. They decided to go to America, where they could have their own kind of worship.

New Lands in America. In 1628, a group of rich Puritans met at Cambridge, England, and formed a company. They prepared to found a colony in America and wanted a large number of people to join this colony. They promised free land in America to anyone who wanted to settle there. This was a wonderful offer to many Englishmen who could never be rich enough to own land in England. Hundreds and hundreds of people packed their few possessions and prepared to leave for America.

Because the Puritans planned to found a colony on Massachusetts Bay, they called themselves the *Massachusetts Bay Company*. In Indian language, Massachusetts means "near the great mountain." The Indians living in Massachusetts were also called by the same name.

The first group of settlers was led by John Endicott. In 1628 he landed on the northeastern coast of Massachusetts at a place called Salem. Salem means "peace." The Puritans had permission to settle on these lands as far west as the **257**

Pacific Ocean. Do you think they realized how large a piece of land that really was?

Boston Is Founded. In 1630 nearly a thousand people came in eleven ships and settled along the Charles River. This river had been explored and named by John Smith in 1614. The settlers called the place Boston, after a city in England. Boston in England had first been called "St. Botolph's Town." Botolph was an Irish monk who lived in England many years ago.

The Largest Colony of England. Between 1630 and 1640, twenty thousand people came to Boston Harbor. When there was not enough land for all these people, some of them moved on to start another settlement a short distance away. Twenty-two towns were soon established in the colony, among them Roxbury, Watertown, Dorchester, and Newtown (now Cambridge).

John Winthrop of England became the first governor of the Massachusetts Bay Colony. The new towns were ruled by Puritans. Many people in these towns did not live up to their new religion. Other people who were not Puritans came and settled in these towns. They came because they hoped to earn an honest living in America for their families. These people were not wealthy, but were willing to work hard for their daily bread.

TOWN LIFE

Governor Winthrop set aside fifty acres of land **258** as pasture land for the colony. Here every farmer could feed his cattle. Today this land is like a big park in the city of Boston. It is called "Boston Common." The little colonial army used the Common as training grounds also. In the Common there was a ducking-pond. If a woman scolded her husband or broke the Sabbath Law she would be ducked in the pond as a punishment.

There are no signs of pasture land today in Boston Common, and there are no soldiers practicing there. But the ducking-pond still remains.

New England Towns. Other towns were built around a little park called a "green," or "common," as Boston was. Every town had its own minister, teacher and meeting-house. The Puritans used the meeting-house for religious services as well as for town meetings. In it they stored away their ammunition for safe-keeping.

Around the open square, the colonists built their homes of pine, maple, and hickory from the forests. These homes were quite close to one another, not miles and miles apart as were those of Virginia. Can you tell why?

The rich Puritans had the first choice of places where they could build their homes. They thought that riches were a sign of God's blessing. The Puritans were wrong about this. Whether we are rich or poor, we please God only when we love and serve Him faithfully.

On Sundays, the Puritans walked to church in groups, just as the Pilgrims did. The Pilgrims did not think it proper to kneel in church. They sat down on long benches that were separated from each other by partitions, or wooden walls. The minister of the meeting-house was one chosen by the people. If they disliked him, or if they disliked his ideas about religion, they could remove him.

The Town Meeting. The Puritan towns governed themselves by holding town meetings. Many New England towns still govern themselves the same way today.

All the people of the town assembled in the meeting-house. They would discuss improvements in the town. They would also elect officers, such as

260 trustees, and men to take care of school matters.

Anyone could come to this meeting and speak about these things. However, only the Puritans could vote. They made their own laws and decided on their own taxes.

The New England town meeting was very important. At these meetings no one represented the people. No one had to speak for them. The people came to the meeting, and each one spoke for himself. This kind of government is called pure democracy. This love of freedom was not a new idea. It was the result of Christian teaching.

After a while, the number of colonists became very large. Then the *General Court* in Boston was formed to make laws.

This was something like the House of Burgesses in Virginia. Each town sent two men to represent it at the General Court.

LIFE IN THE COLONY

Making a Living in New England. The colonists were hard-working people. The men cut and shipped much wood to England, where it could be sold at a good price. After a while, they built their own fishing and trading vessels. In less than fifty years, three hundred sailing vessels which they built were sailing on the blue waters of the Atlantic Ocean. These ships were some of the best and fastest on the ocean.

In 1632, the first ship made in New England shipyards was launched. The ship was named *The*

Blessing of the Bay. The ships made in New England were as strong and swift as any that sailed the seas.

In 1660, England tried to keep the colonies from trading with any other country except herself. The colonies objected to this. This was the beginning of the trouble that was to end in war many years later.

Witchcraft. Many of the early colonists had strange ideas. Some of them believed that certain people were witches. They thought these witches helped the devil in his work. A law was passed making death the punishment for witchcraft.

In 1692, mysterious things happened in the village of Salem. Some children began acting very strangely. An old woman was accused of bewitching them, and was put into prison.

Soon other people were accused of being witches. Many innocent people were imprisoned or put to death for being witches. When it was too late, the governor and people discovered that innocent people had been murdered. The trials for witchcraft died out in Massachusetts.

PURITAN SCHOOL DAYS

Schools for Puritan Boys and Girls. The early leaders of the colony were educated men. Governor Winthrop had studied at a famous college in England. The colonists wanted their children to go to school.

Children were sent to school so they could learn to read the Bible. Many of the older boys continued going to school until they finished college. Most of them did this so they could become Puritan ministers. Some places in New England had private schools. Only wealthy children could afford to go to these schools.

In 1642, the Massachusetts General Court passed a law which ordered every parent in the colony to send his children to school. Many towns then built schools. Five years later, another law commanded every town of fifty families to have a primary school. A town with one hundred families had to have a grammar school. These grammar schools were something like our high schools today. The students in these schools had to study very hard and long.

In 1635, John Harvard, a minister in Cambridge, gave some of his own land and half of his library to start a college. This college was called Harvard College. It was the first college in the English colonies.

The first high school was opened in Boston in 1635. Because Latin was given as a special subject, it was called a *Latin School*. English, and other languages were taught also.

At first, only boys went to school, but later girls were sent too. School began at seven or eight o'clock in the morning and closed at four or five in the afternoon. Lunch-time was from eleven to **263** one o'clock. History, geography, drawing, and music were not taught. If boys and girls knew how to read, write, and do arithmetic problems, they were considered properly educated in the primary school.

Some of the teachers were not well prepared and received very little pay. They used the birch rod whenever pupils failed in their lessons.

The schools were little log cabins, with dirt floors. The pupils had heat in winter only if their parents sent some pine logs for the fireplace. They had no desks. They sat on long wooden benches without backs. There were no blackboards, maps, or pencils. The children wrote on sheets of birchbark with a goose feather pointed at the end.

Schoolbooks. In those days there were no textbooks for small children. Each child had a small wooden board with a short handle. A piece of paper was fastened to the board. On this paper was the alphabet, the numbers 1 to 9, the Lord's Prayer, and a blessing with the words of the sign of the cross. The paper was covered with a thin, clear piece of cow's horn to protect it from damage. It was called a "hornbook."

When the child knew all that was in the hornbook, he was given a book called the "New England Primer." This primer had no beautiful pictures in it or easy stories to read. In it were a few prayers, spelling lessons, questions and answers about the Bible, and the alphabet in rhyme.

Next to each letter of the alphabet was a little picture. After the primer, the pupil was given the Protestant Bible. He not only had to read this but he had to study it as well.

In 1639, the first printing-press was set up in the colonies. In these early days, there were no newspapers. A man called the "town crier" walked through the streets ringing a bell to gather the people in one place. Here he would read from letters or tell them the news of the day. Later, in 1704, the "Boston News Letter," was printed. This was the first newspaper in the colony.

Trouble with England. In 1684, King James of England was afraid that the New England colonists were becoming too powerful. He took the charter away from those who held it. He made Andros their governor, and joined all the New England colonies, New York, and New Jersey under one rule.

The Massachusetts Bay colonists rebelled against this unjust act against their rights as freemen. Armed men gathered in the streets of Boston. Some of the more daring of these men marched to Fort Hill, where Governor Andros lived, and forced him to surrender. Soon after this he was sent back to England.

This rebellion was something like Bacon's Rebellion in Virginia. For a time, the people of Massachusetts again enjoyed their liberty.

A Royal Colony. In 1691, much against the

wishes of the colonists, Massachusetts Bay became a royal colony. That means it was ruled by a governor appointed by the King of England. However, it still kept the General Court and the town meetings.

Plymouth was joined to the colony, as one of its towns. The land which is now Maine was also added to the Massachusetts Bay Colony. This land, Maine of today, remained part of Massachusetts until 1820.

A few Catholics had come to America with the Puritans. However, there were no Catholic priests appointed to care for them. Once, a French priest from Maine came as a guest of an English friend in Boston. This priest, Father Gabriel Druillettes (drew-ee-yet'), secretly offered the Holy Sacrifice of the Mass. This is the first time that the Holy Sacrifice was offered in Boston. Boston today is a very Catholic city.

Helping Your Vocabulary to Grow

Puritan	Separatist	hornbook
Pilgrim	compact	primer
town meeting	meeting-house	partitions
General Court	usher	expel
homespun	succotash	launched

Checking Up on the Facts

Be sure you know the answers to these questions:

1. Which people had the most freedom in the Massachusetts Bay colony?
2. Name three friendly Indians in the Plymouth colony?

3. Tell in your own words just what the Mayflower Compact was and why it is important.
4. Write five sentences telling about the landing of the Pilgrims.
5. When did the Massachusetts Colony accept a governor sent by the King?
6. Give three reasons why Massachusetts Bay Colony became the largest in population.

Talking Things Over

1. Where would you have preferred to live in 1700, in Williamsburg, Quebec, or Boston? Give reasons.
2. Why were Plymouth settlers grateful to God in 1621?
3. Tell the many ways in which your school is different from the early schools in England.
4. Why was Massachusetts Bay Colony a more important colony than Plymouth?
5. Compare the Plymouth colonists and those of Jamestown?
6. Why were New England town meetings important?
7. How did the Pilgrims remain on friendly terms with the Indians for the first fifty years?
8. Compare Governor Winthrop and Governor Bradford as leaders.

Map Work

1. Find on the map, page 320, the Massachusetts Bay Colony in 1691. Draw a map similar to this on your paper. Color the section of Massachusetts Bay Colony that became the state of Maine in 1820.
2. Locate Salem and Boston on this map. Reread the chapter, if necessary, to find something about each these places.
3. On an outline map of the United States, fill in with straight lines or color, if you wish, the land of Virginia and Massachusetts.

CHAPTER IV

ENGLISH CATHOLICS IN MARYLAND

A Land of Freedom. The people who colonized Massachusetts and Virginia were not Catholics. They were either members of the Church of England or had broken away from that church.

One of the English colonies was founded by a Catholic. In this colony, both Catholics and Protestants were allowed to worship God in their own churches. Is this allowed in America today? Do you mean that one religion is as good as another when you say that people can worship God in their own churches?

But Maryland did not enjoy her freedom throughout the colonial days. When the King seized the colony in 1689, things were changed. Catholics had to pay taxes to support the Church of England. They had to pay a fine if they did not attend the Protestant church on Sunday. It was one hundred years later that the new nation, the United States of America, gave freedom of religion to everybody in our country.

268 Maryland is sometimes called the colony of

"Toleration and Tobacco." After you have read the chapter, you may decide for yourself if this is a good name for the Maryland colony.

CALVERT THE CATHOLIC

While Charles I was King of England, a Protestant nobleman named George Calvert lived at Court. George Calvert began to compare the teachings of the Catholic Church with those of the Church of England. He prayed and studied very hard. Soon he became a Catholic.

Calvert was a very good friend of the King. When he became a Catholic he thought he would lose the King's friendship. The King did not turn against him. Although he did not keep Calvert at Court, he gave him a present of a large estate in Ireland, named the *Baltimore* estate. Ever afterwards, Calvert was called Lord Baltimore.

Failure in Newfoundland Colony. The Catholics in England were suffering very much because they remained loyal to the Catholic faith. Lord Baltimore wanted to do something to help them. He obtained permission to start a colony for them in Newfoundland.

Newfoundland had been a favorite fishing ground for the French and English sailors for many years. However, none of these sailors had ever gone there to live.

When the Catholic colonists arrived in Newfoundland, they found the place very cold and **269** almost covered with ice. The winter climate was very severe. The settlers were forced to leave this place. This attempt to found a colony for persecuted Catholics was a failure.

Some of the members of this group tried to settle in Virginia. But the Protestants made them feel unwelcome. So the Catholics returned to England.

Catholics in Maryland. Again King Charles gave land to Lord Baltimore for a colony for Catholics. This land was north of the Virginia colony. Lord Baltimore allowed members of the Church of England to live in his colony. The new colony was called Maryland. Maryland today is truly part of Mary's Land, the Land of Our Lady.

Just at this time, Lord Baltimore died. His son Cecil (ses′-il), was now called Lord Baltimore. The King gave Maryland to the second Lord Baltimore.

Maryland's Charter. In the charter for the colony, it was written that Lord Baltimore could rule the land as his own. He could collect taxes and coin money, but all laws were to be passed with the consent of the colonists.

There was still serious trouble about religion in England. Because of this, Lord Baltimore thought he should stay in England as a protector for the colony. He would be its owner, but he appointed his younger brother, Leonard, as governor.

Bearers of Freedom. On a November day in 1633, two ships left an English port for America. One was named the *Ark,* the other was named the *Dove.*

The Ark stands for the Catholic Church. Do you think that was a good name for a ship carrying freedom-loving people to our land?

The Dove is the symbol of the Holy Spirit. The

Holy Spirit must have helped these Catholic people on their way to this land of freedom.

After about three months at sea, they reached the shores of Chesapeake Bay. One hundred fifty years before, Spanish Catholics had called it "Bay of the Mother of God." The English started their colony near the mouth of a small river near the Bay. The place was very high and very healthful. **271**

It was Our Lady's Day, March 25, 1634, when the settlers started their little colony, which they named St. Mary's. Immediately after landing, they chopped down a tree, made a large cross, and set it up with a little ceremony and procession. There were two Catholic priests with the group, Father Andrew White and Father Altham. Father White celebrated Holy Mass that day. This was the first time the Holy Sacrifice of the Mass was offered in the English-speaking colonies.

Maryland brought to America a greater religious freedom than either Virginia or Massachusetts Bay before her. People of all religions could worship as they pleased in Maryland.

A HAPPY HAVEN

Indian Friends. From the beginning, the Indians were friendly with the Maryland settlers. The colonists treated the Indians with justice and kindness. The Indians sold them some of their cornfields. About half of the Indians moved out of their own cabins to let the settlers live in them. The Indian chief promised to give the settlers more cabins later on. These examples show how kind the Indians were to the first settlers of Maryland.

The colonists paid the Indians with hoes, axes, and other farm tools and useful goods. These tools helped the Indians to do better farming. The colonists paid fair prices for the furs which they bought from the Indians. When an Indian was accused of a crime, he was never savagely punished. He was treated with justice.

As a result of the friendliness of the Indians, the Maryland colonists enjoyed peace. They did not have to keep their guns loaded in fear of Indian attacks.

Calvert was very friendly to the Indians. He wanted them to have lands of their own, where they could live in peace. He set aside certain lands for the Indians. No white man might settle on these lands. The lands which were set aside for the Indians were called *reservations*. Governor Calvert placed Jesuit priests in charge of these reservations. The Maryland colony was the only English settlement that made such plans for the peace and happiness of the Indians.

Life in Maryland. Each colonist received two thousand acres of land. In return for this land, the settler had to pay a small part of whatever crops he raised. Many workers were needed. Indentured servants soon came to the Maryland colony. As these servants gradually became landowners, more and more Negro slaves were forced to do the work of the fields.

Since the soil of Maryland was not good for raising corn and wheat, tobacco became the chief crop, as it was in Virginia. This brought great wealth to Maryland settlers because tobacco sold at a high price in England.

Another reason why the Maryland colony was **273**

so successful from the beginning was that the colonists could buy chickens, hogs, and cattle from the Virginia colony, instead of bringing them from England. As a result, Maryland grew more in six months than Virginia did in six years.

Although their houses were far apart, the Maryland plantation owners built real homes.

These brave and fearless people had come to stay. They were willing to work hard to develop the land that gave them freedom of worship and a peaceful family life.

RELIGIOUS FREEDOM

Maryland offered religious freedom to anyone who lived there. However, not many Englishmen chose to live there. They loved their native England, and did not want to leave it.

Since Lord Baltimore also offered religious freedom to everyone, many people of other religions came to live there. A thousand Puritans came from Virginia. These Puritans started a settlement at the place that is now Annapolis (an-a'-po-lis), but which they called Providence. Other Puritans and some Quakers came from England, and Protestants came from Germany to settle in Maryland. The colony soon became a place of safety and refuge for all other persecuted peoples, besides Catholics.

A Famous Law. Trouble was going on in England between the King and the Puritans. The Maryland colonists wondered if the Puritans would try to take away their freedom of worship. To prevent this, Lord Baltimore asked the colonists to pass a law.

Now they would write down the wishes of the colony's owner, Lord Baltimore. Not only Catholics could practice their religion freely, but all who believed in Jesus Christ could practice their religion in the colony. Although Lord Baltimore was a Catholic, he did not force other people to attend the Catholic church. He permitted other religions to exist in the colony.

We call this way of looking at things *toleration*. The new law that was passed at this time was called the *Toleration Act of 1649.*

275

Troublemaker of the Colony. Later, trouble came to Maryland. The colonists were divided in their loyalties to the different parties waging war in England. Governor Calvert naturally favored the King, but the Puritan settlers sided with the English Parliament.

A Puritan from Virginia, named William Claiborne, decided to make trouble in Maryland. He persuaded the Puritans to fight against the Maryland government, and drive the Catholic priests out of the colony.

In the midst of all this, Governor Calvert died. Lord Baltimore appointed a Protestant as the new governor of Maryland. This governor also believed in toleration. Still the Puritans were not satisfied.

Claiborne's party finally put an end to the government. They cast aside the Toleration Act and made a law allowing only Puritans to hold church services. We say that the Puritans repealed the Toleration Act. They also sent word to Lord Baltimore that he had no claim to the colony.

For four years the Puritans ruled the colony. Then Lord Baltimore received his colony back in 1657. Once more the Toleration Act became law in Maryland, and the colonists had freedom of worship again.

A Royal Colony. All freedom of worship was taken away from the colonists in 1692 by King William and Queen Mary, who were Protestants.

276

Lord Baltimore's colony was taken away from him, and made a royal colony.

Under this plan of government, all the Maryland colonists had to support the Church of England. No Catholic was allowed to enter the colony. Those who were already living there were forbidden to vote or hold any office. If a priest was found offering the Holy Sacrifice of the Mass, he was sent to prison for the rest of his life. This was a sad end for a land that began with the spirit of religious toleration.

Maryland became one of the states belonging to the United States of America in 1788.

Catholics in Maryland. We have read how the colony of Maryland was founded by Catholics. We also saw how the Catholics were later forbidden to practice their religion.

The laws forbidding Catholics to practice their religion were passed by men who did not like the Catholic Church. These men did not love the Blessed Mother. They did not have the right idea of what God wanted men to do.

Even though there are such people in the world, it is the duty of Catholics to pray for them and ask God to help them to see the truth. Catholics must not persecute such people, even though they are wrong. We must be kind to everybody.

New Words to Learn

proprietor	repealed	friendliness
toleration	reservation	

Clinching Our Ideas

Try to answer these questions without taking another look at the chapter:

1. To what colony did Maryland belong before 1634?
2. Show the difference in the kind of freedom granted by the House of Burgesses, the Mayflower Compact, and the Toleration Act.
3. In which colony would you have preferred to live in 1650?
4. Why did England claim all the land along the coast as hers?
5. Name the important dates studied so far in this unit.

Keeping Up with Our Work

1. Dramatize the sections of this chapter which tell the chief events in the life of Lord Baltimore.
2. Pretend you were present at the first Holy Mass offered in Maryland. Write a letter to a friend in England telling why this was an important act.
3. Discuss the following points with other pupils in your class.
   a. Why did the Toleration Act not give complete religious liberty?
   b. If England was a Protestant country, how did it happen that a colony was founded for Catholics?
   c. How did the Church of England become the religion of the Maryland colony in 1691?
4. Write an acrostic based on the word *Maryland*.
5. On an outline map of the thirteen colonies show the various products made in Virginia, Massachusetts, and Maryland. Do this by drawing symbols on the map for the articles represented.

CHAPTER V

LET FREEDOM RING!

Looking Over the Chapter. You have just read about the three English colonies in America. Each of these was founded by men of different religions. The Anglicans founded Virginia. The Puritans came to Massachusetts Bay. Catholics were the early colonists in Maryland.

Fifty years after the cross was placed on the soil of Maryland, people of still another religion came to start a colony. They were called Quakers. They came from England and other colonies to live in Penn's Woods, or Pennsylvania.

The history of this colony tells of Penn's love for all his fellowmen, whether they were white men, black men, or red men. The freedom of religion in his colony attracted many people. The Dutch, Germans, Swedes, Irish, and Scots came to enjoy religious freedom. Because of this, Penn's colony began to grow rapidly.

This chapter is the story of William Penn's founding of a colony in the year 1682.

WHILE the Pilgrims were starting their colony at Plymouth, a young shepherd boy named George Fox was tending his sheep on the hillsides of England. In his spare moments he read his Bible, which he carried with him wherever he went.

As he read the Bible, young George Fox thought a great deal. He decided that people would be very much happier if they obeyed Christ's command to love one another. Do you agree with him in this?

Another New Religion. George Fox talked to his friends about his ideas. Later he and his friends formed a little group and called themselves the Society of Friends.

These men believed that all men were equal and no one deserved more respect than any other. Because they believed this, they refused to take off their hats to anyone, even to the King.

These people refused to take oaths, even lawful ones. They did not believe anyone should go to war. Since they did not believe in the Church of England, they refused to pay taxes to support it. Besides, those taxes helped support the army and navy.

This Society of Friends built meeting-houses without steeples or decorations of any kind. When the people came to meeting they would sit in silence for a long time, thinking deeply about God. **280** They had no ministers. When someone in the group thought of something that might help others live better, he would rise and tell it to the others. They called this practice "following the inner light."

The Friends dressed very plainly, in gray, brown, or other quiet colors. They did not wear gay and fashionable clothing. They did not want to be proud of their clothes.

A New Name for the Friends. One day George Fox disturbed the services in another church. He was arrested and brought to court. Still wearing his hat, George Fox stood looking straight at the judge. He said to the judge, "I bid thee *tremble* before the word of the Lord." The judge answered, "I bid thee *quake* before the law!" From that day on, the Friends became known as Quakers.

Penn Becomes a Quaker. William Penn was a student at Oxford University, which is a famous university in England. He heard of the Quaker religion, and made up his mind to join it.

After Penn became a Quaker, he refused to go to the university chapel because it belonged to the Church of England. The students and teachers at this university wore special gowns. Penn refused to wear his and tried to stop others from wearing theirs. For this he was expelled from the university.

William Penn's father was a brave and skillful admiral in the English navy. He was greatly displeased to learn that his son was expelled from **281**

Oxford University. He had hoped to see his son become a great navy hero like himself. He begged his son to change his religion, but William refused to obey. His father drove him out of his house.

Land for Quakers. King Charles had spent more money than he should. As a result he borrowed much money from others. William Penn's father loaned the King $80,000. When Penn's father died, the King owed the money to William Penn.

Penn thought of a plan. He knew the King owned many rich lands in America. He would ask the King to give him some land in America in payment of his father's debt. On this land, he could start a colony where people of all religions could worship God as they pleased.

The King gladly agreed to Penn's request. He gave him a piece of land north of Maryland. Penn wanted the land named "Sylvania," which means *woodland*, but the King changed the name to Pennsylvania in honor of William Penn's father.

IN PENN'S WOODS

In 1682 William Penn sailed up the Delaware River, looking for a place to settle on his own lands. Many Swedes had settled at a place called Upland. Penn changed the name of this town to Chester, but allowed the Swedes to live there undisturbed.

Farther up the river, Penn found a suitable

place to settle. He named it *Philadelphia,* which means brotherly love. The first thing he did was to lay out a plan for the city.

Up to this time, no other city had been planned in any colony. The colonists had been allowed to build their homes wherever they pleased. This was

a poor arrangement because the streets went in zigzag fashion.

William Penn planned his city well. In the center, space was reserved for public buildings. All the streets formed squares. Is your school on a street that crosses another street?

Penn's Laws. Penn found some other settlers besides the Swedes living on the land that was his. **283**

He thought they should all know about the laws he had made for them. Therefore, soon after landing, he called a great meeting of all the people in Pennsylvania.

Penn's set of laws was called the Great Law. This law allowed all who paid taxes to vote. Each person could worship God in his own way.

According to this law, only two crimes, murder and treason, could be punished by death. Schools were established, and every boy had to learn a trade.

Indians and Penn. The Indians in Pennsylvania at that time were the Iroquois in the north, and the Algonquins in the south. Soon after his arrival, William Penn held a meeting with these Indians.

The Indians came to this meeting wearing their war paint. They brought with them bows, arrows, and heavy spears. They were prepared in case the white men might attack them. Penn and his men had no weapons, but sat down in a friendly manner.

Penn told the Indians that he wanted to be their friend. He said he would never make war on them, nor carry guns. He promised to treat them fairly. He would not take their land by force, but he would buy it from them if his people needed it.

The Indians told Penn, "So long as the sun and moon shall shine, the Indians and the English will **284** live together in love and peace." Penn said, "We will be brethren, my people and your people, as the children of one Father."

This was a very famous treaty. It proved that people of different races and nations can get along in peace and harmony, when each side has the good-will to do so. As long as Penn was alive, the Indians and the colonists got along well and had no trouble of any kind.

After William Penn died, the Englishmen were not just in their dealings with the Indians. This famous treaty was then broken.

New Settlers. Although Pennsylvania was settled long after most of the other colonies, it grew much faster than any of them, except Massachusetts Colony.

In many countries of Europe, people were persecuted because of their religion. Wars also caused great suffering at this time. Therefore, many thousands of families gratefully accepted Penn's invitation to make their homes in his colony.

After two years in the New World, William Penn returned to England to settle some business. It was fifteen years before he returned to his beloved colony. He remained another two years, but was then called back to England again. He never returned to his colony or to his own family, who lived all this time on a large estate beside the Delaware River.

Catholics in Pennsylvania. In the early days, there were very few Catholics in Pennsylvania. 285

Once in a while, Catholic priests from Maryland and New York visited them. After some time, a number of German Catholics came, and with them a few Jesuit priests.

In 1731, the first Catholic parish, St. Joseph's, was started in Philadelphia.

How Harrisburg Started. About twenty years after Penn landed, an Englishman named John Harris crossed the ocean and settled in Philadelphia. After a while he moved farther west and built his house on the banks of the Susquehanna (sus-kweh-han′-a) River.

Near his house, the river was shallow. At some parts of the year people could wade across it. Harris found this spot a good place to trade with the Indians.

Later, John Harris's son began to carry men and their goods across the river in a flatboat, or ferry. This made Harris' home and lands more valuable. Soon a large town grew around Harris' land. Finally, this land became the city of Harrisburg, the present capital of Pennsylvania.

MASON AND DIXON LINE

When the King of England granted charters to his people to start colonies in America, he did not set the exact boundary lines of the colony. The reason for this was that very little was known about the amount of land in America.

No one knew the exact southern boundary of

Pennsylvania. Nor did anyone know the exact northern boundary of Maryland. Both colonies claimed some of the same land. Quarrels started between these two colonies and continued for over fifty years.

In 1763, two English surveyors named Mason and Dixon were hired to set the exact boundary.

LORD BALTIMORE.   WILLIAM PENN.

You can imagine how difficult it was to do this. The men climbed over mountains and through deep forests. At every five-mile space, they put up a stone pillar with Lord Baltimore's coat-of-arms on one side and William Penn's on the other. This line of markers was called the Mason and Dixon Line. Later, it became the dividing line between the free and slave states.

Growing in Word-Mastery

Quaker	valuable	loyalties
flatboat	surveyors	persuaded
shallow	admiral	

Things to Discuss and Study

1. Why were there fewer towns in Virginia and Maryland than in the North?
2. Why was Pennsylvania a good place for a Catholic to live after 1690?
3. Compare the religious freedom found in Maryland and the kind of religious freedom found in Pennsylvania.
4. Why did Penn invite all persecuted people to his colony?
5. In what way did William Penn practice kindness to the Indians?

Pulling Together the Threads of the Unit

1. Prepare a dictionary file of all the new terms you learned in this unit.
2. Dramatize William Penn's meeting with the Indians.
3. Write a paragraph of at least four sentences about the Mason and Dixon line. Read it to the class at the next meeting of your history club.
4. On an outline map of the colonies show the difference between the borderlines of the four colonies studied, and the states today. You may do this by coloring one line blue and another red.
5. Draw a poster such as Penn might have sent to Europe to invite people of all countries to his colony.
6. Make a booklet describing the work of Penn, John Smith, Governor Winthrop, and Lord Baltimore.
7. Make a scrap-book of pictures and stories about the four colonies studied. When you have finished

Unit Five, you will add to your collection stories and pictures of the nine other colonies.

8. Make a simple map of your own, showing the land owned by the English and colonized by them. Color the parts you have learned about already. As you progress in the next unit, color the other colonies as you study about them.

9. Write a paragraph on one of the chapters of this unit. Turn to the outline on page 203 for help in remembering the important facts on the chapter you select.

UNIT FOUR — MASTERY TEST

I. On your paper write "Yes" or "No" to the following questions:

   a. Were town meetings a good way of practicing democracy?

   b. Did Plymouth colony join Massachusetts Bay colony?

   c. Did Maryland colony become a Crown colony?

   d. Did Penn live peacefully with the Indians?

   e. Were the Puritans members of the Church of England?

   f. Was George Calvert a Catholic?

   g. Was Plymouth the first English colony in America?

   h. Could everyone in the Massachusetts Bay colony vote?

   i. Did Massachusetts pass laws about building schools?

   j. Did people in Massachusetts live like the people in Virginia?

   k. Is William and Mary College older than Harvard?

II. List these events in the order in which they took place:

Pennsylvania founded

Tobacco first grown in Virginia

Mayflower Compact written

Act of Toleration

Drake's trip around the World

    Do the same with the following:

Cabot's explorations

First Negro slaves in English colony

Penn's "Great Law"

Mason and Dixon Line

The first Thanksgiving Day

III. Copy the names of the following colonies on your paper. Write after each, the number accompanying the correct answer below.

      Virginia

      Massachusetts

      Maryland

      Pennsylvania

Sample: The first college, built in 1635. (The correct answer is Massachusetts. Place "1" after Massachusetts above.)

1. The first college, built in 1635.
2. All religions could worship God in their own churches.
3. Where Harrisburg is located.
4. Named after Queen Elizabeth.
5. Where Catholics could worship God freely until 1689.
6. Where only Puritans could vote.

7. The first body of lawmakers met.
8. Founded one year before Quebec.
9. Owned by Lord Baltimore.
10. Where each child learned to read from a hornbook.
11. Where slavery began.
12. Where Drake stopped and took on all colonists as his passengers.
13. Where the "City of Brotherly Love" is located.
14. Trials for witchcraft took place.
15. Where John Smith saved his life.

IV. On another sheet of paper, write the answers that correctly fill in the blanks:

1. The leader of a rebellion in Virginia was _____.

2. The nobleman who tried to start colonies and failed was _____.

3. The chief of the Massachusetts Indians was _____.

4. Town meetings were first held in _____.

5. William Penn brought the religion of the _____ to America.

6. The only colony where freedom of worship was permitted by 1700 was _____.

7. The law passed in Maryland in 1649 was called _____.

8. The representatives from the different settlements in Virginia formed the _____.

9. A colony owned directly by the king is called a _____ Colony.

10. The capital of Virginia was later moved to _____.

V. Match the following groups of words in Column A with Column B. Copy the first line under "A" and complete the sentence with the words in "B."

A	B
1. an indentured servant	stricter than the Church of England
2. Puritan	made to work for another
3. Quakers	agreed to work for another
4. Cavalier	the Friends
5. a slave	loyal to King of England

VI. Answer these questions on your paper in full sentences:

1. Why did Queen Elizabeth knight Sir Francis Drake?

2. Why was the Mayflower Compact a greater step towards freedom than the House of Burgesses?

3. In which colony could a Catholic go to Mass on Sunday?

4. Name three important events that occurred in 1619.

5. Name some Cavaliers who brought honor to Virginia.

6. Name three colonies that enjoyed the friendship of the Indians.

UNIT FIVE

ROUNDING OUT THIRTEEN

CHAPTER I—CONQUERED BY CAPTURE

Henry Hudson explored the waters north of Europe.

The French and English claimed parts of the New World.

Henry Hudson explored the Hudson River in 1609.

The Dutch settled Manhattan and founded the colony of New Netherland.

Henry Hudson discovered Hudson Bay.

The English captured New Netherland in 1664.

Governor Dongan became the English governor of New York.

The Charter of Liberties was passed as a law for New York.

New Jersey and Delaware colonies were later formed from New Netherland. **293**

CHAPTER II—MORE NEW ENGLAND COLONIES

Roger Williams disagreed with the Puritans.

Rhode Island was founded by Roger Williams in 1636.

Mrs. Hutchinson founded the settlement of Portsmouth.

The Fundamental Orders of Connecticut were adopted.

Thomas Hooker founded the Connecticut Colony.

The Charter of Connecticut was saved from the English.

Land north of Massachusetts Bay later became the colony of New Hampshire.

CHAPTER III—SOUTH OF VIRGINIA

The King of England gave all land from Virginia to Florida to eight of his friends in 1663.

Albermarle County was founded.

The King divided the land into North and South Carolina in 1729.

Forest products were a source of income to the settlers.

Georgia was founded in 1733, from land that was part of South Carolina.

Oglethorpe helped unfortunate debtors from English prisons.

UNIT FIVE

ROUNDING OUT THIRTEEN

IN UNIT FOUR we read about the colonies whose first settlers came directly from England in the seventeenth century. These four colonies were important. They grew to be "little England" in America.

After some time, England got more colonies in America. The Dutch had settled on lands along the coast between the southern colonies and Massachusetts Bay. England conquered these lands in 1664. By doing this, she added three more colonies, New York, New Jersey, and Delaware, to those she had. How many colonies had she then?

Settlers from Massachusetts Bay Colony moved south and north of her boundaries and formed separate colonies. The new colonies were New Hampshire, Rhode Island, and Connecticut.

England extended her southern boundary line to Florida and gained three colonies by doing this. The first settlers of the Carolina land had come from Virginia, where they were discontented. The Carolina land later became the colonies of North Carolina, South Carolina, and Georgia.

The colonies were growing. New York and

Philadelphia became important seaports. Most of the trade between the colonies, and trade to Europe passed through these ports. Boston and Charleston also became important.

Most of the people lived along the seacoast and in river valleys. Most of them also lived on farms. Virginia and Massachusetts had the largest number of people living in their colonies, with Pennsylvania ranking third.

These English colonists brought to America the love for liberty. They spread it in this great land, our own United States of America.

We shall read in this unit about the settlement of some of the largest colonies of the thirteen.

We shall see how the Dutch lost the colony of New Amsterdam to the English, and how this colony came to be called New York.

We shall learn about one of the great governors of New York, Thomas Dongan, who was a Catholic. Under Governor Dongan's rule many wise laws were passed for the colony.

The other colonies of New Jersey and Delaware were later formed from the colony of New York.

Then we shall read about colonies further south, and how they were established. These colonies became very wealthy because of their products.

All the colonies we shall read about in this

chapter became States of the United States.

CHAPTER I

CONQUERED BY CAPTURE

Looking Over the Chapter. Every boy and girl knows that today New York is a very important city. But about three hundred years ago it was only a small village where little Dutch boys and girls in wooden shoes went clitter-clatter down the crooked streets. Tidy Hollanders also lived along the Hudson River and around Albany.

Indian wigwams and trading posts were here and there on this land.

The Dutch lived in neat brick houses. The warm sunlight came in through the spotless windows of their kitchens.

For forty years the Dutch flag of orange, white, and blue waved over the forests and settlements of New Netherland, as the colony was called.

Then, one day in 1664, the flag of the colony was changed to the English flag. The English captured the colony without a single shot having been fired. The Dutch continued to live there, but under English laws and government.

The story of the New Jersey and Delaware **297**

colonies is also connected with the English capture of New Netherland. This land belonged to the Dutch before the English King gave it away as though it belonged to him.

In this chapter you will read the interesting story of how the Dutch lands became an English colony. You will read how this colony grew until New York became the second largest city in the thirteen colonies of America.

HUDSON'S TRIPS

AFTER Spain lost control of the seas in 1588, another nation, the Dutch, began exploring. Holland once belonged to Spain. When she became independent of Spain she became powerful on the seas. In order to increase her trade, she too wanted to discover a shorter route to the East than the one around the Cape of Good Hope.

The Dutch people lived on the lowlands in the northwestern part of Europe. They had become rich and famous by trading with foreign countries. They owned several islands in the East Indies. From these islands, they obtained pepper, cloves, and coffee which they used for trade.

The little seaside country where the Dutch people lived was called Holland, or Netherland. Although this country was small, its people occupied a great amount of land throughout the world.

A Hired Captain. One of the famous companies
started by the Dutch for trading with other na-

tions was the Dutch East India Company. An English sea captain, who worked for this company, was commanded to find a northeast route to the Indies. This Englishman was Henry Hudson.

Hudson's ship looked like a large house of many colors floating on the sea.

It was a very fine ship, and Henry Hudson was proud of it.

The ship was painted in bright colors. It carried the flag of Amsterdam, the flag of the Netherlands, and the flag of the Dutch East India Company. Hudson called his boat the *Half Moon*.

When Hudson started out from Holland, he headed north. Then he looked east for a passage by which he could reach Japan. He met the cold, frozen waters of the North, which stopped him from going any farther. Instead of turning back to the Netherlands, he sailed west across the Atlantic.

Brave Henry Hudson knew he was making a daring trip. Many others before him had tried this and failed. When he reached the New World, he first entered Delaware Bay, but soon turned back. He thought this water was much too shallow to be a route leading to the Pacific Ocean.

He continued north up the coast and found a very deep bay and a very deep river. As he sailed up the river, he noticed the thick forests on each side of the river. Hudson knew then that the land was very fertile and rainfall abundant. Groups of Indians stood together here and there on the shore. They were frightened as they saw the gaily painted ship sailing up the river.

As Hudson sailed on, he discovered that the river grew more and more shallow. After sailing about one hundred fifty miles up the river, he realized that this waterway was not a passage to the Pacific Ocean. However, he called the river by his own name. It is still called the Hudson River. The year was about 1609.

Henry Hudson made friends with the Iroquois Indians on his first voyage to the New World. The Dutch were very glad that Hudson had made **300** such friendly acquaintances along the Hudson

River. Before leaving, he traded axes, beads, buttons, and clothing in exchange for furs, tobacco, corn, pumpkins, and grapes.

At the Turn of the Century. South of the Hudson River, the first English colony was just about started. North of the Hudson, the French were making a claim on Quebec. Because of Henry Hudson's voyage, the Dutch also claimed a piece of land in the New World.

All this happened in the early days of the seventeenth century. 1607, 1608 and 1609 are very important dates. Dates beginning with the numerals 16 belong to the seventeenth century.

Farther south, below Virginia, there were people from Europe too. You learned in Unit Two that these people were the Spaniards. But they had been exploring our lands for about a hundred years. Their first colony was founded in 1565. You remember how the Spanish lost many of their lands after the defeat of the Armada.

Ask your teacher to let the class prepare a discussion on "America at the beginning of the seventeenth century." Be sure you can locate on your map the sections of land each country claimed for itself.

Hudson Sails Again. The trip up the Hudson River was the only trip Henry Hudson made under the Dutch flag. Later, Hudson sailed much farther north, under the English flag. He sailed past Labrador and went on until he discoverd such a large bay that he thought surely it was the Pacific Ocean. This bay is still called Hudson Bay.

When he sailed southward on the bay, he came upon a land of ice and snow, and not the land he was looking for. It was so cold that his ship froze in the ice. When the warm days of springtime melted the ice, his crew cruelly put Hudson in a small boat to drift away by himself. They took his ship, and sailed for England. Henry Hudson was never heard of again.

IN OLD MANHATTAN

WHEN Hudson returned to Holland from his first trip to the New World, the Dutch merchants were happy to see the rich furs and other articles he had obtained from the Indians. The merchants formed a new company, called the Dutch West India Company. The government hoped this company would increase the wealth and trade of the country. The Dutch government gave the company the right to start settlements in the New World.

A "Heavenly Land." The first Dutch colonists settled along the Hudson River and on the little rocky island at the mouth of the river. This island was called Manhattan by the Indians. Manhattan means "heavenly land." It lies between the North and East Rivers.

The Dutch called the island "New Amsterdam," **302** but the whole colony was called New Netherland.

They also built a trading post far up the Hudson River. They called this place Fort Orange. It stood at the place where the city of Albany now stands.

Peter Minuit (min'-you-it) was sent by the company as the first Dutch governor in 1626. He decided to rule the colony from Manhattan. A settlement had already been started on an island in

the bay near Manhattan. Manhattan Island had only a few Indian tents scattered here and there.

A Famous Purchase. Peter Minuit thought it was unjust to take the island because it really belonged to the Indians. So he bought it from them. He gave them twenty-four dollars' worth of beads, trinkets, knives, and a few other articles. The Indians prized these articles very highly. Today, that twenty-four dollar island is worth billions and billions of dollars because it is part of New York City, the second largest city in the world.

Although Minuit was a good governor, the directors of the Dutch West India Company did not think he was making enough money for the company. Therefore, in 1631, they forced him to return to Holland.

PATROONS IN NEW NETHERLAND

IT WAS hard for the Dutch West India Company to get the Dutch people to leave their homes in Holland and go to a strange country. To coax people to come to America, the company worked out a plan. Large estates in New Netherland were offered to some rich men in Holland, if they could get fifty Dutch people to come to America. The owner of the estate would have full charge of these fifty people. In other words, the rich owner was their patron; in Dutch you would call him *patroon.*

Many of these patroons never came to America. They had their people working for them in America. So long as these colonists sent the patroons the furs and other products they wanted, they were satisfied.

These workers received no pay from their masters. However, they had to pay rent for their land, and pay for use of the mill for grinding grain. These colonists were bound to work for the patroon for about ten years. Indentured servants were treated better than the colonists of the patroons.

Of course, the patroon had to pay the Indians for the land he occupied. He also had to give his fifty colonists houses, land, cattle, and tools. Besides, he had to provide a minister, a schoolmaster, and a mill for grinding corn.

Famous Patroons. Because of this patroon system, many fine old Dutch families made their homes on large estates in New Netherland. One patroon owned all of Staten Island. The Van Rensselaer (ren'-se-ler) estate near Albany was another very large estate. Van Cortlandt owned 85,000 acres around what is now Van Cortlandt Park in the Bronx. Other important patroons were the Schuylers (sky'-lers) and the Roosevelts.

It was on the Van Rensselaer estate that Saint Isaac Jogues found refuge when he escaped from the Iroquois Indians.

The patroon system did not please the simple Dutch people. It gave them little freedom. They were refused the rights which God intended them to have as human beings. For this reason, very few Dutch people brought their boys and girls to America to live.

OLD SILVER NAILS

THE chief business of the Dutch in New Netherland was fur trading and farming. The people who lived around New Amsterdam became shipowners. **305**

They carried the goods of the colony to other lands. New Amsterdam was growing into a large city. Its people were busy and industrious.

The colonists, however, were not satisfied with the governors sent them by the trading company. Governor Van Twiller, who came after Minuit, favored the patroons, rather than the poor people.

He was called back to Holland, and Governor Kieft (keeft) became governor. He made even stricter laws than the former governor. The settlers had to pay a tax on goods shipped out of the country. Anyone found selling guns to the Indians was to be put to death.

A Governor's Nickname. In 1646, a new gover-

nor arrived. His name was Peter Stuyvesant (sty'-
ve-sant). He was a man who had a very strong
temper and received the nickname "Headstrong
Peter." This tall, heavy, well-dressed man had lost
his right leg in a battle some time before. In its
place he wore a wooden leg, with silver bands and
rows of shiny silver nails upon it. He received another nickname, "Silver Nails." The two nick-
names seemed to fit him very well.

Governor Stuyvesant was not a bad ruler by
any means. He worked for the good of the colony,
and built schoolhouses, new homes, and forts.
Many people now came to settle in the colony.
These people came not only from different countries of Europe, but even from the nearby English colonies.

Still the people did not like Peter Stuyvesant.
He fretted and scolded wherever he went, as he
stumped about on his silvery wooden leg. When
the colonists asked for greater freedom, he was
quite harsh with them.

Peace with the Indians. During Stuyvesant's
time, some Dutchmen were unjust in trading with
the Indians, and there was trouble. The governor
very wisely sent some of his men to make a peace
treaty with the Indians. He warned his colonists
to be more just and kind to the Indians in the
future.

In order to fortify the settlement against any
further attack, Stuyvesant had a twelve-foot wall, **307**

or palisade, built. It was made of pointed logs and fitted with gates. Just inside this wall there was a street. The wall has long since disappeared, but the street is still there. It is named Wall Street. The largest banks of the world are on Wall Street today.

Settling a Dispute. In the early days, the Dutch spread out to the east of Manhattan as well as to the north. They settled as far east as Hartford in Connecticut. The English from Massachusetts Bay Colony had made settlements in the Connecticut River Valley. Both the Dutch and the English claimed the same land. In order to settle this dispute, Stuyvesant traveled to Hartford in 1650. A boundary line was agreed upon between the New England and Dutch settlements. That boundary line is almost the same as the present one between Connecticut and New York. The Dutch were not pleased with the settlement of this quarrel. They thought the Puritans were allowed too great a share of lands.

A NEW FLAG OVER THE HUDSON

THE Dutch colony grew very quickly. It also made much money from shipping and trade. All this caused England to become jealous of it. Except for Florida, it was the one place along the Atlantic seacoast which did not belong to her. What do you think England did about it?

A Famous Letter. One day in 1664, the English

sailed into the harbor of New Amsterdam. Colonel Nicolls, their commander, had a letter for Governor Stuyvesant. In this letter, the Dutch were told that the land on which they were living belonged to England. The Dutch had been colonizing on this land for forty years. Now the English came to claim it for themselves. They claimed it because John Cabot had explored the coast of North America almost two hundred years before.

When Peter Stuyvesant read the letter from the English King, he became very angry. In a rage of temper, he tore the letter into pieces and threw them on the floor. He said he would rather die than give up New Netherland to the English.

The Dutch people asked Stuyvesant what message was in the letter. The governor made no reply. Then they picked up the pieces of paper from the floor. They put the pieces together and read the message. To their surprise, the English were offering them rights which the Dutch West India Company had refused them. The letter also said the English would allow them to keep their own property, as well as their churches, if the Dutch would give up the colony to the English.

England Rules. The Dutch surrendered to the English. Not a shot was fired. Now the Dutch could share the freedom of the English colonies.

Holland lost her lands in America. The Dutch people, however, kept their homes, lands, and language. The English flag waved over the Hudson. All the land along the Atlantic coast, except Florida, now belonged to England. The English King then gave the colony to his brother, who was the Duke of York. The Duke of York was free to rule these lands as he wished.

The New Netherland colony included also land which forms the states of New Jersey and Dela-

ware today. The Dutch had erected trading posts south of New Amsterdam, but they had not made strong settlements there. Later in this chapter you will read about the way the Duke of York divided this land among various other English people who brought settlers to America.

Stuyvesant was sent to Holland, but after a few years he returned to his lands in New York.

His farm in New York was called *"bouery,"* after the Dutch word for farm. Part of Stuyvesant's farm later became part of the *Bowery,* a famous street in New York.

NEW YORK IN EARLY DAYS

CHANGES of all kinds took place in the Hudson River Valley after the English took it over. The Duke of York changed the name of the colony to New York. This duke had another title, the Duke of Albany. Fort Orange was changed to Albany. Many places in New York have kept Dutch names to this day. Do you know any of these names?

Washington Irving, a writer, has told many delightful stories about the customs of the Hudson River Valley residents. Every boy and girl loves to hear of the ghosts, goblins, and the headless horseman that lived in New York long ago. The custom of expecting Santa Claus at Christmas has come down to us from the Dutch people. Did you know that doughnuts were a favorite Dutch food?

Government in New York. Colonel Nicolls became the first English governor. He made a set of laws for the colonists, called "Duke's Laws." They were not so harsh as the former Dutch laws. However, the people were not allowed to be represented in a legislature, as in other English colonies.

England and Holland were at war in 1673, and Holland again took over the colony of New York. **311**

But, after the treaty of peace, the land became English property again.

Edmund Andros was sent to take charge of the colony in 1674. He did one important thing. He appointed a committee to keep friendship between the English and the Iroquois Indians.

Andros had much trouble with the people because they did not like the heavy taxes. The Duke of York recalled him and sent a very fine Catholic gentleman named Thomas Dongan, to take his place.

DONGAN'S RULE

GOVERNOR DONGAN was a good and wise governor. All the time that he was governor, the colony was successful and advanced in many ways.

The first act of Dongan was to hold a meeting of seventeen representatives chosen by the people. The purpose of the meeting was to pass laws for the good of the colony. This Assembly, which met in New York City, was the first of its kind in the history of the colony.

In order that the people might be more fairly represented in the Assembly, Governor Dongan divided the land in the colony into counties. He divided the land in as equal a manner as possible. Each county was allowed one representative in the Assembly. Each county had its own officers to run the affairs of the county.

312   A Great Document. While Dongan was governor some very good laws were passed. This set of laws was called the Charter of Liberties. This charter called for a meeting every three years to settle the question of taxes. All who were not slaves could vote. Trial by jury and freedom of worship were guaranteed by this charter. It was signed by the seventeen members of the Assembly and then sent to the Duke of York, who approved it. This meant that the charter then became the official law of the colony.

This Charter of Liberties was a sign of a great freedom that was soon to come. It was a great step towards the freedom that was to be born in America.

Freedom Only for a Time. The freedom given by this Charter of Liberties did not last long. In 1685 the King of England died, and his brother, the Duke of York, became king. His name as king was James VI. He was the first Catholic king England had had for almost one hundred fifty years. As king, the Duke of York had authority over all English colonies, not just over New York.

For some unknown reason, he called Governor Dongan back to England. He refused to allow the New York colony to use the Charter of Liberties. It was used in the colony only two years. But this Charter of Liberties was later used as a guide in drawing up the Constitution of the United States.

Dongan's Treaty with the Indians. Before Dongan had left his office as governor, he made a very important treaty with the Iroquois Indians. He did this in order to prevent the French from capturing New York. In this treaty, which the Indians signed, they called the King of England their Great Chief.

Because the Indians had claimed the King of England as their head, the English later claimed all the land used by the Iroquois tribes. In this way, all the land that is now in New York State fell into the hands of the English.

Discontent in New York. After Dongan left, matters in the colony went from bad to worse. The New Yorkers were forced to join the newly-formed Dominion of New England. All the colonies North of Pennsylvania were united as one. Only the King could make the laws. Andros was appointed governor for all. The colonists were not satisfied with this. They lost all their freedom. This made them dislike the King of England.

Excitement in England. In England, King James displeased the people so much that they drove him from the country. They placed his daughter Mary, and her husband, Prince William of Orange, on the throne.

New York was happy about this change in England. The colonists too took things into their own hands. They seized Andros and put him into prison.

In New York, at that time, there was a rich merchant named Jacob Leisler (lye'sler). He took control of the government and called the Assembly. The Assembly gave him almost full power to govern.

Leisler governed for two years. In 1690 a ship from England brought a new governor to the colony. Jacob Leisler refused to surrender the fort. For this action, he was tried for treason and executed. From this time on, New York was ruled as a Crown Colony of England.

New York was one of the first thirteen states forming the United States of America, after the Revolutionary War.

NEW JERSEY

AT FIRST, New Jersey was part of the New Netherland colony. When the English captured New Jersey in 1664, it became part of the New York colony.

The King of England gave the entire New Netherland colony to his brother, the Duke of York. The Duke of York gave some land away in 1676. This land lay between the Hudson and Delaware Rivers. It was called Jersey after the Island of Jersey in the English Channel.

Sir George Carteret received the eastern part of the Jersey land. Lord Berkeley received the western part.

Lord Berkeley's Section. Many Quakers came to live in West Jersey. After some time, a few of them bought Lord Berkeley's land. It was later sold to some other men who were Quakers. One of

315

these Quakers was William Penn. You have already studied about William Penn in Unit Four.

Sir George Carterets' Section. East Jersey was first governed by the nephew of Sir George Carteret. He ruled the colony well. In 1664, some people came from Long Island, New York. They started a settlement called *Elizabethtown* in East Jersey. The next year some Puritans from New Haven, Connecticut, founded *Newark*.

In 1682, twenty-four Quakers bought East Jersey for $17,000. One of these Quakers was William Penn.

Land of Quakers. Now both East and West Jersey belonged to the Quakers. After a while it came under the rule of the King of England. Later it was given back to the Quakers. In 1702, the two sections were joined together as one colony, New Jersey, which belonged to the King. It had its own assembly, but it was ruled by the governor in New York. New Jersey was allowed to elect its own governor for the first time in 1738.

DELAWARE

Three Flags over Delaware. The Dutch settled south of Delaware Bay in 1631. The Indians destroyed this settlement later.

In 1638, some Swedish people settled on the same land. Their leader was a man whom you have met before in this chapter. He was the former Dutch leader, Peter Minuit. He had joined the

Swedish army after he returned to Holland.

The new colony was named New Sweden. A fort was built to protect the colony. This fort was named Christina, after the young Swedish queen at that time.

Minuit was drowned in 1638, and the colony had no governor for the next five years. Then the Dutch came back and captured New Sweden. The Swedish people did not like this. They fought against the Dutch. The Dutch had seven warships and seven hundred soldiers. The Swedes had neither. The Dutch won. It was 1655. Now the Dutch ruled the Swedish settlements.

England captured all the Dutch colonies in 1664. The Duke of York gave a new name to the land where the Swedish people lived. He called it *Delaware,* in honor of an Englishman who had explored that land. *New Castle* was made the capital of Delaware. This Swedish section remained part of the New York colony.

Part of Pennsylvania. William Penn had his eyes on Delaware. Pennsylvania land had no seacoast, so Penn bought Delaware and united it to Pennsylvania in 1682. This plan did not work out well. The people of Pennsylvania and Delaware did not agree.

After 1702 Delaware was allowed to have an assembly of its own. Later still, it was allowed to elect its own governor. Then it was recognized as a separate colony. How many English colonies **317** have you studied so far? Which do you think is the most important?

Can You Define These Words?

captured	New Amsterdam	estate
fertile	patroon	Bowery
provided	directors	industrious

Things to Do

1. Instead of making a new time-line for this unit, it would be more interesting to add the new dates you have learned in this chapter to the time-line you have already made for Unit Four. In this way, you will have a complete time-line of the thirteen colonies by the time you have finished this unit.

2. Locate on the classroom map the following places: Newark, Albany, New York City.

3. Why have many places in New York kept Dutch names?

4. Discuss whether or not it was right for England to capture New Netherland.

5. State two important events connected with each of the following: Dongan, Minuit, Leisler, Stuyvesant, and Andros.

6. Name three colonies that were once owned by Quakers.

7. Look up more information about New York Colony. Compare Manhattan today with Manhattan in the early days of the Dutch settlers. Your encyclopedia will tell you many interesting things about this topic.

8. Dramatize the Fall of New Amsterdam in 1664.

9. Compare the life of a workman for a patroon with the life of an indentured servant.

Check-up on English Colonies

A. Fill the blanks with the name of a colony.

1. The Puritans first lived in _____.
2. The largest colony in population was _____.
3. English Catholics founded the _____ colony.
4. Tobacco was first raised in _____.
5. The Duke of York gave _____ to two of his friends.
6. Because Pennsylvania had no seacoast, Penn bought _____.
7. The Dutch were the first to live in _____.
8. In 1619 Negro slaves first came to _____.
9. Town meetings were first held in _____.
10. In 1649 the Toleration Act was passed in _____.

B. Fill the following blanks with the name of a prominent colonial person.

1. _____ bought Manhattan.
2. A Catholic governor of New York was _____.
3. The English forced _____ to surrender New Netherland in 1664.
4. John Smith's life was saved by _____.
5. The first governor of Plymouth Colony was _____.
6. Ever since the founding of his colony, _____ allowed freedom of worship in Maryland.
7. _____ made a famous treaty with the Indians in 1682.
8. The Indian chief who was friendly with the Puritans in Massachusetts was _____.
9. The governor appointed to take charge of all colonies north of Pennsylvania in 1686 was _____.
10. The people of Virginia rebelled against injustice, under the leadership of _____.

CHAPTER II

MORE NEW ENGLAND COLONIES

Looking Over the Chapter. You have read about the beginning of the Massachusetts Bay Colony. Three other colonies were founded in the Northeast by people who first lived in the Massachusetts Bay Colony.

A young minister was put out of the Massachusetts Bay Colony. He traveled southward and began a settlement which he called Providence. Three other settlements were made close to Providence. Taken together, they became known as the Colony of Rhode Island and Providence Plantations.

Another settlement was made by a minister from Massachusetts Bay Colony. Thomas Hooker set out towards the south with his followers. This settlement and other nearby settlements later formed the Connecticut Colony.

Some people made their homes along the coast north of Massachusetts Bay. The colony in time became known as the New Hampshire Colony.

This chapter completes the story of the four English colonies that settled in the northeastern **320** part of the present United States.

IN THE early days in Massachusetts Bay Colony, there lived a young man named Roger Williams. This man was the minister of a Puritan meeting-house in Salem. He was a friend of the Indians.

According to the law of the colony, every minister had to preach the Puritan ideas of religion to the people.

Roger Williams' Ideas. Roger Williams had some ideas on religion that were not the same as those of the other Puritans. He believed that the land in the colony really belonged to the Indians. He said the colonists should have paid the Indians for the land before settling there. He thought that **321**

all the people in the colony should be allowed to vote, not the Puritans alone. He believed that no one should be forced to support a church when he did not belong to it.

Roger Williams dared to preach his own ideas in his meeting-house on Sunday mornings. The Puritan men and women were very strict about what they believed. His teachings displeased the members of his congregation very much.

Kindly neighbors tried to make Roger Williams change his mind. They warned him that he was getting himself into trouble. Roger Williams did not listen. He believed he was right and would not change his ideas for anyone.

The Puritan leaders in Boston decided to put Roger Williams out of the colony. They ordered him to leave for England on the next boat.

Roger Williams made no move to obey this command. If he should go to England, he knew he could not preach his own ideas of religion there. He knew he could not stay in Salem, either.

Leaving the Colony. He thought of starting another settlement some other place. In the middle of winter he left Salem and fled towards the south. He went on until he came to an Indian settlement. Here kind Indians sheltered and cared for him until springtime.

This Indian village really belonged to the Indian chief, Massasoit. The Plymouth colonists also **322** claimed this land. They were angry when they heard that Williams was living there. They ordered him to leave this land at once.

Roger Williams was on the road again. He traveled many more miles southward. Finally, he reached the upper shores of Narragansett Bay. Here, with some companions he met along the way, he made a settlement. He called it *Providence,* because of God's Providence in watching over him. Can you find Providence on your map? (Page 320).

Williams was not the first to visit this land. Verrazano stopped there in 1524, and the Dutch explorer, Adrien Block, explored it in 1614.

Nearby Towns. In the Plymouth colony there lived a Puritan named Mrs. Anne Hutchinson. She had different ideas than the Puritans. When she spoke openly against the Puritan religion she was expelled from the colony.

In 1638, she went south and settled on an island near Providence. She called the name of her settlement *Portsmouth.* The next year, on another corner of this island, a settlement was made. It was called Newport. Five years afterwards, the name of the island was changed from Aquidneck, its Indian name, to "Rhode Island."

There is another story about the name of the colony. As far back as 1614, some Dutch traders called the place "Red Island" because there were so many cranberries there. After a while "Red Island" was changed to Rhode Island.   **323**

A settlement was made at Warwick in 1644. Then there were four settlements quite close to one another.

A Colony Is Formed. Roger Williams had some trouble in the beginning, because Massachusetts Bay Colony also claimed his land. He asked the King of England for a separate charter for his colony. In 1647, Providence, Portsmouth, Newport, and Warwick were united into one colony. The colony was called "Rhode Island and Providence Plantations." In this title the word *plantations* means *colonies*. Even today, the state of Rhode Island keeps the name "Rhode Island and Providence Plantations."

Roger Williams was chosen leader of the colony. He began to carry out his ideas about justice and charity. He paid the Indians for the land on which he made his settlement. He said it belonged to them.

Everyone was allowed to vote in his colony. No one had to support a church to which he did not belong. Everyone could attend whatever church he desired.

Roger Williams was not a Catholic. On the contrary, he was the first to found the Baptist Church in America.

In 1663, another charter was granted to the colony. It gave the colonists more freedom. However, only people who owned a certain amount of property could vote. It remained the charter of the colony until 1843, when another set of laws went into effect.

A law was passed in Rhode Island in 1719, forbidding Catholics and Jews the right to vote. This law was not fair or just.

Rhode Island was one of the English colonies which broke away from England in 1776.

CONNECTICUT

THE land south of Massachusetts Bay Colony had been discovered by the Dutch in 1613. These people paid the Indians for this land. In 1633, they built Fort Good Hope on this land.

But the English King claimed the land, too. He gave that same land away to some of his friends in 1632. In this grant of land, it was stated that the land extended from the Atlantic to the Pacific Ocean.

Both Holland and England claimed this land. Do you remember from Chapter One of this unit how Peter Stuyvesant made a boundary line between New Amsterdam and Connecticut? In the end, the Dutch had to give the land to the English.

First Permanent Settlement. In Cambridge there lived a Puritan minister named Thomas Hooker. He was discontented in the Massachusetts colony.

He heard about rich farm lands that were some distance south, along the shores of a river. The Indians called this river "Connecticut," or long river. The Dutch traders called it "Freshwater **325**

River." The Connecticut River flows through the state of Connecticut, from north to south, and empties into Long Island Sound.

Early Connecticut Towns. Hooker thought this land would be a good place to start a colony of his own. In the year 1636, Hooker led a group of people southward from Cambridge. For two weeks the weary travelers marched on through the forests until they reached the banks of the river.

The first settlement was made at Windsor. Later, Hooker moved farther south and established Hartford. A settlement was also made at Wethersfield.

A New Colony and a Written Law. In 1639, the people got together to form a colony. This colony was known as Connecticut. The people formed this colony without the permission of the King of England.

Each little settlement sent representatives that year to a meeting in Hartford. The purpose of this meeting was to make laws for the colony. The laws that were drawn up at this meeting were called the *Fundamental Orders of Connecticut.*

These laws were very important because they were the first written set of laws in a colony in America and gave the people a freedom greater than that of the Massachusetts Bay Colony. The people could elect their own governor and representatives. However, the governor had to be a **326** member of the Puritan Church.

Other Settlements. In 1648, a very strict group of Puritans settled on Connecticut lands. They called their colony New Haven. Some members of this colony came directly from England, others from Massachusetts. Only members of the Congregational Church could vote. Their laws were very severe and harsh. Other towns were established along Long Island Sound.

In 1662, the people of Connecticut thought it would be wise to ask the King of England for a charter for their colony. Up to this time, they had no charter. The charter was finally granted. It allowed the colonists to keep the rights they received from the Fundamental Orders of Connecticut. By this charter, New Haven was united with Hartford and the other settlements into one colony.

The people could elect their own governor and representatives. However, those elected to office had to be members of the Congregational Church. They had all the rights of English citizens.

The charter came from England in a handsome mahogany box. The charter was beautifully decorated and had a picture of King Charles II on it. You may see this famous charter sometime when you visit Connecticut.

Hiding the Charter. A later king, James II, decided to take all the charters away from the colonies. The people of Connecticut refused to give up their charter. The King sent Edmund Andros **327**

to take the charter by force. This was in 1687. Do you remember where you read about Governor Andros before?

When Andros came to the Assembly Room, the representatives received him politely. Andros told them his errand. The members started to talk

to him about something else that was not so important.

In the meantime, it was getting late. Evening came, and the candles were lit. Then the long box containing the charter was brought in. It was placed on the table before Andros.

He was about to take it, when suddenly someone blew out the candles. When the candles were lit again, there was no charter on the table. There was no one missing from the room, either. Andros had to leave without the charter. The people of Connecticut planned all this ahead of time. Do you admire them for acting this way?

A certain captain hid the charter that night in the trunk of an oak tree. This tree was called the "Charter Oak."

In 1688, it was safe to take out the charter, for James II was no longer king of England. The people lived according to this charter for one hundred and twenty years afterwards.

The founding of the Connecticut colony was another step in the great march of freedom. This was a colony of free men living under free laws and constitution.

Connecticut was one of the original thirteen colonies that broke away from England in 1776. It fought for independence and became part of the United States.

NEW HAMPSHIRE

THE colony of New Hampshire was at first part of the land belonging to the Massachusetts Bay Colony. We know that Captain John Smith visited this land in 1614. In 1622, Sir Ferdinand Gorges (gore'-ges) and a merchant bought land from the Merrimac to the Kennebec Rivers.

In 1629, John Mason built a house near a river in the southern section of this land. He and Gorges then divided the land between them. Mason kept **329** the lower half, and Gorges kept the upper region.

Gorges' Section. The upper section, which belonged to Gorges, was known as the District of Maine. It later became part of Massachusetts Bay Colony. Many years afterwards, Maine was governed as part of the Massachusetts Bay Colony. Very much later, in 1820, Maine became a separate state.

Mason's Section. Mason called his portion of land New Hampshire, after Hampshire, England. Settlements were made by fishermen and others at Dover and Hampton. In 1629, Mr. Wheelwright bought some land and founded Exeter.

As long as Mason lived, he owned his colony. Mason died in 1633, and Massachusetts took over the colony of New Hampshire. The relatives of Mason complained about this. Do you think they had reason to complain?

New Hampshire continued to be ruled by Massachusetts just the same. The King of England, James II, decided to settle the matter in 1680. He made New Hampshire a separate colony again. He himself would appoint its governor and those who would assist him. The people, however, could elect their own representatives to make the laws.

New Hampshire was one of the thirteen colonies which formed the United States of America in 1776. It played an important part in the Revolutionary War.

330   **The Growth of Liberty.** We have seen in this

chapter that the people of these colonies all desired liberty. They were all willing to work for it and even fight for it.

It was this desire for liberty that was later to grow into the war for independence from England. We shall read about this war, the Revolutionary War, in the next book in this series.

We can see from this chapter how the idea of liberty and freedom was implanted in the early colonies. It was from ideas like this that the United States of America was born.

Our New Words

mahogany	decorated	relatives
Providence	Dover	Exeter
		Hartford

To Help Us Think Clearly

1. Name the colonies formed by men who first settled in Massachusetts Bay Colony.
2. Tell how Connecticut became a colony which governed itself for many years.
3. Prepare to discuss how many nations could claim Rhode Island because their explorers visited this land.
4. Who had greater claim to Connecticut, the Dutch, who bought it from the Indians, or the English, who claimed it themselves?
5. Give two examples from this chapter showing that the English practiced justice to the Indians.

More Work to Do

1. Locate on the map, page 320, Connecticut, Rhode Island, New Hampshire.
2. Find in your encyclopedia or other history books all you can about those colonies. You can discuss these events in class later.

CHAPTER III

SOUTH OF VIRGINIA

Looking Over the Chapter. So far, you have studied about ten of England's colonies. The colonies you studied about in Unit Four were those founded by people who came from England in the seventeenth century. So far, in this unit, you read about three colonies formed on land that was captured. You found out also that three more colonies were started by people who left Massachusetts Bay Colony.

In this chapter you will study about three colonies founded on land south of Virginia. In the beginning, this entire section was known as the land of the Carolinas.

The first settlers of Carolina came from Virginia. They were not getting along very well there. By 1733, the land of the Carolinas was divided into three colonies, North Carolina, South Carolina, and Georgia. Georgia was settled in the eighteenth century by people from England.

This chapter is the story of the founding of the Carolinas and Georgia. These colonies are known **332** as the Southern Colonies.

Moving South. In 1653, there were some people in the Virginia colony who were not getting along well there. They wished to have better homes, so they got together their few possessions and left the settlement. They moved to lands south of Virginia.

When they arrived at a suitable spot by the side of a river, they halted. They called the place *Albemarle.*

For ten years these settlers lived by themselves in the wilderness. They were ruled by the government of Virginia, and their land was called "Albemarle County."

Lasting Settlement. In 1663, another settlement was founded south of Virginia. Some people came from an English colony in the West Indies. They came from Barbados (bar-bay'-dose) Island. These people paid the Indians for some land beside the river, and built homes near the present site of Wilmington. This land was called "Clarendon County." It extended from Cape Fear to Florida.

This colony grew very quickly. Some of the people who came to the colony had taken part in Bacon's Rebellion in Virginia. This was the beginning of what was later called North Carolina.

Eight Men's Colony. In 1663, the King of England gave eight noblemen the land between Virginia and Florida, and extending westward to the **333**

Pacific Ocean. We call these men *proprietors,* because they were the owners of the land. They named the land Carolina, after King Charles.

Six years later, the proprietors ordered John Locke and another famous Englishman to draw up a set of rules for the colony. These rules were called the "Grand Model," but they were really no model at all. They gave no rights to the people. This was against the plan of God. God wants all men to be treated fairly.

These people could not own their lands, according to the new law. It was not right to make a law like this, for God gave every man the right to own property.

This part of Carolina has a very regular coastline. There is no harbor on the coast. So, when the Carolina settlers wanted to send wheat, corn, tobacco, and fat cattle to England, they had to ship their goods first to a Virginia port.

There were no slaves in Carolina in these early days. There were no indentured servants, either.

Settlements Farther South. In 1670, some colonists moved farther south, below Cape Fear. They, too, were governed by Virginia. The colony was called Count Carteret Colony. These settlers moved a few more times before 1682. In that year they found themselves at the junction of the Ashley and Cooper Rivers. It was here that the settlement of Charleston was founded. It grew to be a very wealthy town of the southern colonies. There was a fine harbor here also, the best one south of Chesapeake Bay.

Soon afterwards, the Dutch made a settlement close by. Some Irish, Scotch, Swiss and German people came, also. In 1690, some French Protestants settled in the southern section of Carolina.

There were many quarrels among these people over matters of religion and politics. Then, too, they suffered from the Indian raids along the coast. Their houses were plundered and robbed, and their lives were often threatened. Life was difficult in these early days.

Settlers who moved to the farther regions of the Carolinas found means of earning their living other than by planting tobacco. They found the land almost entirely covered with forests. Wood from these trees was used in building ships. Other things taken from the trees were pitch, tar, and turpentine. Pitch, tar, and turpentine are called naval stores.

Tar was used to coat the ropes and planks of ships, and also to fill in the cracks. The turpentine was useful in soaking the ropes and rigging of the ships, to make them strong and firm.

They sold these products to the West Indies and to the pirates whose ships lay in the nearby waters. These pirates used to raid the Spanish ships on their way to Europe from America. Later, these pirates treated the English ships in the same way.

335

A Present for the Governor. The southern part of Carolina was very different from the northern part. It was low and damp, with very poor soil. One day about 1680, a Dutch captain gave the governor a present. The present was a bag of rice. The governor planted the rice and found out that this land was just right for raising rice. It grew very well. It brought great wealth and money to South Carolina for many years.

As in Virginia, the colonists of South Carolina began to buy slaves for their plantations. Many more Negroes were needed to work in the rice fields than the people of North Carolina needed for their tobacco fields. England, Europe, and other colonies were the customers of South Carolina. They bought shiploads of rice.

Another Successful Crop. About sixty years later, a girl named Eliza (e-lie′-za) Lucas planted some seeds in her father's back yard. These seeds came from India. They were the seeds of the indigo plant. Eliza found out that the plant grew very well in South Carolina.

The leaves and flowers of this plant were cut and boiled for a long time. A scum was formed which made a rich blue dye. People used this dye to color woolen and cotton goods. The countries of Europe wanted this dye very much. This plant helped to make South Carolina a very wealthy place. It soon became South Carolina's second important crop.

Life in Charleston. Life in Charleston was most pleasant. The planters had large homes, surrounded by beautiful gardens. The planters had many servants who did the work while they went fox-hunting, and enjoyed other sports. The people dressed beautifully and had costly furniture. The town had a library, a theatre, and several

fashionable inns. The children of the planters went to Europe for their education.

Like Virginia, the people had to attend the Church of England and pay taxes towards its support. At first, neither Quakers nor Catholics were permitted to live in the colony. Later, Quakers could live there, but Catholics were still forbidden. **337**

In 1711, the Indians made a sudden attack up-on the English colonists and killed thirty of them with hatchet and knife. They continued on their way, killing as they went along. In 1713, they were defeated and left the colony.

Spain tried several times to capture Charleston Harbor. The colonists were very much displeased because the eight proprietors did not do anything to help protect them. In 1719, the colonists rebelled and elected one of their own men as governor. The King of England approved of their act.

In 1729, the King of England bought back the Carolina land from the eight proprietors for $80,000. The King divided the land into North and South Carolina. Each division was to have its own law-making body and its own governor.

In 1776 these colonies were among the thirteen that declared their independence of England.

THE LAST COLONY OF ALL

WHEN King George II was the ruler of Eng-land, some very harsh laws were passed. One of these laws said that people who owed money could be sent to jail until they paid the debt. In jail, they could earn no money to pay their debts, so many of them stayed there for a long time. Prisons were terrible places, dark holes full of dirt and disease. Many innocent people were left to die in such prisons.

James Oglethorpe, a favorite officer of the

King, had a very dear friend in one of these prisons. When his friend died in prison, Oglethorpe was very, very sad. He made up his mind to do something to help other unfortunate debtors.

Plan for a Colony. General Oglethorpe thought it would be a fine thing if these poor people could get a fresh start in life by moving to some other place. He asked the King for permission to found a colony for them.

At this time there was a great argument or dispute going on between England and Spain about some lands in America. The southern part of the land called Carolina was a dark, dreary wilderness. The English claimed this land as theirs. King Charles II had given it to his eight friends in his charter of 1663. Land from Virginia to Florida was theirs by this charter. After 1729, this land was part of South Carolina.

The Spaniards, too, claimed this land. De Soto had explored it in 1540. Franciscans, as well as Jesuits, had set up Catholic missions for the Indians in that region many, many years before. Catholic Spaniards were in Georgia long before the Protestant English came to America at all.

Oglethorpe wanted to settle a colony on these disputed lands. He brought the first group of debtors to this land. In the spring of 1733, he laid the foundations for his colony on the Savannah River. The people built a fort on a high bluff and called the place Savannah, the Indian name for the river. The colony was called Georgia, in honor of the King.

Oglethorpe laid out the town carefully, almost the same way that Penn planned Philadelphia. First, the trees were cut down. Then broad streets were cut in straight lines. At first the settlers lived in tents. Then log houses were built. This made life much easier for the settlers.

The colony grew very slowly in its early days. The reason for this may be that the colony had rules which were disliked by many people. One law stated that the colonists had to grow certain things, such as silkworms and grapes. These did not grow well on the soil of Georgia.

340   Only men who fought in the army could own

a certain amount of land. They could not sell it to another. Colonists could not own slaves, nor buy strong drink. No Catholics could enter the colony. This law was made to keep the Spanish from making homes in Georgia.

After living ten years in Georgia, Oglethorpe returned to England.

Colony Owned by the King. In 1750, one law of Georgia was changed. The people requested that slaves be permitted in the colony to work in the rice and indigo fields.

Later, in 1752, Georgia colony was turned over to the King, and Georgia became a royal colony. After this, the colony grew rapidly.

Some New Words

indigo	turpentine	debtor
rice	dispute	naval stores

To Help You Remember This Chapter
1. Which colony that you read about in this chapter had poor harbors?
2. Which colony had tobacco plantations? rice and indigo plantations?
3. Find on your map, page 320, Savannah, Charleston, Wilmington. Sketch this map on your paper and print the names of these settlements on your own map.
4. Pretend you were a member of the Charleston settlement in 1729. Write a letter to a dear friend in England, telling about the kind of life you led in South Carolina.
5. Look over the outlines at the beginning of Units Four and Five. Write on your paper the names of the thirteen colonies settled by the English. **341**

High Lights of the Unit

1. Name the Southern colonies; the Middle Atlantic colonies; the New England colonies.

2. Prepare a chart of the colonies listed below. Use the following headings.

First settlers	Reasons for founding	Date of Charter	Date became Royal Colony
Rhode Island			
New Hampshire			
Connecticut			
North Carolina			
South Carolina			
Georgia			

3. Write the following headings on your paper. Fill them in afterwards.

	New York	New Jersey	Delaware
First settlers			
Reasons for founding			
Date captured.			
Date became royal colony			

4. Prepare a pageant. Your teacher will assign each pupil the name of a certain colony. That pupil will prepare a report on that colony. The teacher will assign a day for the pageant to be held. (See manual for further details.)

5. Number the lines on your paper 1 to 10. After each number write S, F, or E, whichever people, Spanish, French or English, answers the statement correctly.

   1. They wanted religious freedom.
   2. They came to trade with the Indians.
   3. They landed at San Salvador.
   4. They looked for gold in the South.
   5. They sailed the Delaware River.
   6. They called the Mississippi "River of the Immaculate Conception."

342

7. They named a settlement "St. Mary's."
8. They opened twenty-two missions for the Indians in the West.
9. They held town meetings and governed themselves.
10. They came from a Protestant country.
6. Arrange in order the following events:
   St. Lawrence River discovered
   St. Augustine founded
   La Salle's trip down the Mississippi
   The first trip around the world
   Hudson River discovered
7. Arrange these in the order in which they were founded:
   Jamestown
   Quebec
   Sante Fe
   St. Augustine
   New Orleans

UNIT FIVE — MASTERY TEST

I. On a separate sheet of paper, write the word or words that will properly fill in the blanks:
   1. A colony was composed of groups of people, each group forming a _____.
   2. The founder of Providence was _____.
   3. Providence and three other settlements together formed the _____.
   4. The District of _____ remained part of Massachusetts Bay Colony until 1820.
   5. New Haven was founded by very strict _____.
   6. Before the English settled Connecticut, the _____ settled there.
   7. People from _____ Colony first made homes in New Hampshire.

8. A colony founded without the king's permission was _____.

9. At first, Carolina consisted of the land forming the present states of _____, _____, and _____.

10. _____ and _____ were the chief crops of South Carolina.

11. Georgia was founded by soldier colonists who kept the other colonies free from _____ attacks.

12. Connecticut's laws were known as the "_____."

13. Rhode Island received a charter from the king in _____ (year).

14. No Catholics were allowed in _____.

15. On Georgia's plantations were raised the same crops as in _____.

16. New York was first settled by the _____.

17. Silkworms could not be raised in _____.

18. Three colonies that were once New Netherland were _____, _____, and _____.

19. Governor Andros ruled for a time all colonies north of _____.

20. The colony of Georgia was formed from part of _____ land.

II. Write on your paper the numbers 1 to 10. After each number write the name of the colony or colonies connected with each name below.

1. Pocahontas
2. Thomas Dongan
3. Oglethorpe
4. Thomas Hooker
5. Stuyvesant
6. Roger Williams

7. Minuit

8. Mrs. Anne Hutchinson
9. William Penn
10. Jacob Leisler

III. Place these events in the order in which they occurred:
   a. Georgia is founded
   b. Rhode Island is founded
   c. North Carolina is founded
   d. Dutch settle Manhattan
   e. Connecticut is founded

Do the same with these:
   a. First English colony founded
   b. First Spanish settlement in U. S.
   c. First Dutch settlement
   d. Quebec founded
   e. First Mass in English colonies

IV. Select the correct answer from the choices below, and write the answers on a separate sheet of paper.
   1. A colony founded for protection against the Spaniards was: *a)* Maryland; *b)* Rhode Island; *c)* Georgia; *d)* Pennsylvania.
   2. New Netherland became the property of the English when: *a)* Henry Hudson claimed it; *b)* the king of England took it; *c)* the first settlers arrived; *d)* Lord Berkeley purchased it.
   3. The first settlers of Rhode Island came from: *a)* England; *b)* France; *c)* Holland; *d)* an English colony.
   4. How many colonies were finally formed from the land first called Carolina? *a)* one; *b)* two; *c)* three; *d)* four.
   5. Governor Dongan was a: *a)* Quaker; *b)* Puritan; *c)* member of the Church of England; *d)* Catholic.

345

6. The Charter of Liberties was a set of laws made for: *a*) Connecticut; *b*) Carolinas; *c*) New York; *d*) Rhode Island and Provience Plantations.

7. A patroon is one who: *a*) owned some of the lands in the Dutch colony; *b*) came to New Netherlands to work; *c*) served as an army officer of the Dutch; *d*) helped to capture the Dutch colony.

8. After 1700, a Catholic could live peacefully only in the colony of: *a*) Maryland; *b*) Pennsylvania; *c*) Virginia; *d*) New York.

9. The chief kind of freedom that the English brought to America was freedom: *a*) of speech; *b*) to rule oneself; *c*) of the press; *d*) to do as one pleased.

10. A proprietor is one who: *a*) governs the colony for another: *b*) rules the colony from England; *c*) has ownership of the colony; *d*) seizes the colony and rules it.

V. Answer these questions in complete sentences.
1. Explain the difference between a patroon and a slave.

2. Which two colonies had freedom of worship in the beginning?

3. Which were more important, and why: the laws of the Carolinas, or those of Connecticut?

4. If you lived in 1700, where would you have preferred to live, in the southern colonies, or the New England colonies? Give reasons for your answer.

5. Name the Spanish colonies in America in 1733; also those of France and England in that year.

UNIT SIX

FRENCH LANDS IN ENGLISH HANDS

CHAPTER I—DIVIDED ENGLISHMEN

The French, English, and Spanish owned land in America in 1750.

France and Spain had few colonies in the New World.

France and England were at war for almost a hundred years.

The Engish captured the French colony of Acadia.

Some settlers from Acadia came to Maryland.

In America both the English and French colonists claimed the same piece of land.

The French denied English claims to the Ohio Valley.

The French tried to take the Ohio Valley from the English.

The English built forts in the Ohio Valley.

The French refused to give up the Ohio Valley.

The English fought the French and were defeated.

England openly declared war on France.

The English colonists would not unite to fight against the French.

Franklin proposed a plan of union.

CHAPTER II — UNITED ENGLISHMEN

George Washington was an officer in the English army.

Braddock was defeated.

The French won most of the battles until William Pitt sent large armies to help the colonists.

The English captured Fort Duquesne and called it Fort Pitt.

The English won battles in New York State.

Quebec fell in 1759.

Peace was made in 1763.

At the end of the French and Indian War, France lost all her lands in America.

The Spanish lost Florida.

The French and Indian War resulted in bringing the colonists closer together.

Franklin was an important man in the colonies.

UNIT SIX

FRENCH LANDS IN ENGLISH HANDS

WE HAVE watched the Spanish, French, and English settlers build their cabins and their colonies in different parts of young America. Many English colonists came to America. They were seeking freedom of worship and better ways of supporting their families. The freedom they sought and found in America made this land very dear to them.

We have seen how America has grown and the reasons why so many settlers came. But, in the early days, there was no unity among them. Each of the English colonies had its own ways of doing things and governing itself. With freedom within their own colony, the people had no need of looking for it elsewhere.

The soil and the climate were different in each of the colonies. Lumbering, fishing, and trade gave the people in New England a good living. In the South, the plantations brought riches to the people living there. The products of the wheat and cornfields of the Middle Atlantic colonies earned for them the name of the "Bread Colonies."

England was still "home" to many settlers, and **349**

they still loved the land of their birth. Naturally, when a war started between France and England in 1689, they were on the side of England. If France won, what would become of their lands, their homes, the freedom they loved?

In the first three wars that followed, between France and England, no great change was made on American lands, except that England won Acadia and Newfoundland from the French. The colonies were still content to be living under the flag of England.

We shall see one of the important things that came out of the early struggles between France and England. This was the plan drawn up by Benjamin Franklin. It was called the *Plan of Union.*

This plan was very important because it was the first attempt to get the people of all the colonies to work and fight together.

Franklin's plan, however, was not successful. The people of America were still too much interested in their own colonies to work together.

Later on, we shall see that the people of the colonies began to work together as Americans, not as members of the separate colonies.

The story in this unit tells us about the way colonists began to realize that "in union there is strength."

It was this lesson they were to put into practice in the Revolutionary War.

CHAPTER I

DIVIDED ENGLISHMEN

English and French in America. When war started in Europe in 1650 between France and England, it was to last for almost one hundred years. This war was carried to the colonies, too.

The French and English began to build forts in the Ohio Valley. The French refused to give up the land to the English. Open war followed.

In this chapter you will study about the lands gained by the English in 1713, and the dreadful events that followed in Acadia. You will also study the difficulties that arose between English and French colonists, and the refusal of the English colonists to unite against a common enemy.

TWO NATIONS AT WAR

America in 1750. A glance at the map on page 352 will give you a good idea of the way our land was divided among three nations in 1750.

Spain had a fairly large portion of land in the South.

France had plenty of waterways to her credit. The St. Lawrence River, the Great Lakes, and the Mississippi River were claimed by France, as well **351** as the lands surrounding these rivers and lakes. It is very true to say that the French were the "river farers" of America.

Stretching down along the coast of America on the East is a strip of land. This land was owned by England. Every now and then, from 1607 to 1733, people came from England and built homes in America.

We must remember, too, in studying this map that France and Spain had very few colonies in America. These countries had much land, but few people. England had little land in America but that land contained many people.

France and England at War. Things were going along well among the colonists of the three nations in America. But trouble started in Europe in 1689. A war broke out between England and France. This war lasted for more than a hundred years. Sometimes there were short periods of peace, but most of the time the two countries were at war.

COLONIES AT WAR

SINCE France and England were at war in Europe, their colonists in America began to fight each other also. The French attacked the English, and the English often raided French forts and settlements. The Indians took part in these wars, too. The Iroquois were on the English side, and the Algonquin Indians fought with the French.

352   The wars fought between the colonists in

America were called *intercolonial* wars. They are known as King William's War, Queen Anne's War, and King George's War.

Results of Wars. Very little change was made on the map of America on account of these wars. When Queen Anne's War was over in 1713, Acadia

was taken from the French and given to the English. Newfoundland also became English property at this time.

THE SAD FATE OF ACADIA

WHEN Acadia fell into the hands of the English, many loyal Frenchmen left the homes they loved to find peace elsewhere. The intercolonial wars were not yet over, and there was a greal deal of unfriendliness among the colonists of both nations. Do you think these colonists should have been unfriendly towards each other?

French Catholics Suffer. The new governor of Acadia ordered the Acadians who remained to take the oath of allegiance to the King of England. You must remember that the King of England was also head of the Church of England. These loyal Acadians refused to do this because they were Frenchmen and Catholics.

Because of the refusal of the Acadians, the English did a very cruel deed. They had all the settlers of the little village of Grand Pré (gran pray) gather in their humble country church. Here they were told they were to be expelled from their land.

Six thousand Frenchmen, young and old, were forced on English boats which took them to different places in the English colonies. Children were separated from their parents. Wives never saw their husbands again.

After some time, some of the people found their families in Louisiana or in Canada, but the greater number of them never did. Longfellow, a poet, has told the sad story of two separated lovers in his poem "Evangeline."

Nine hundred of these people were admitted to the Maryland colony. A group of them started a

Catholic chapel in Baltimore. This chapel was the

beginning of Baltimore's Cathedral of the Assumption of Our Lady.

What do you think of the way the English treated these French Catholics?

England changed the name of Acadia when she took it over. After 1713, Acadia was called Nova Scotia, which means "New Scotland."

THE COLONIES CLASH AGAIN

THIRTEEN colonies with thirteen governments, and almost as many different religions, were located along the Atlantic coast of America. They were happy because of the freedom they enjoyed. This freedom was such as they had never known in the Old World.

These people owned more land than that on which they made their homes. When they were coming to the New World, the King of England had given them charters for lands from the Atlantic to the Pacific Oceans. However, the colonists were not in any hurry, in those early days, to explore the lands they really owned farther west.

As the years went on, the colonists began to push westward. They crossed the mountains and built new homes on the other side.

When the colonists crossed the mountains in Pennsylvania, they found that their lands were very close to the French settlements. These lands were important, they knew. Indians had told the English about the Ohio River to the west of the **355**

Allegheny Mountains. This river flowed southwest until it emptied into the great Mississippi River. Can you tell why this made the land around the Ohio River important?

The Ohio Company of Virginia. Some men in Virginia heard about the rich lands in western Pennsylvania. The King of England gave them a grant of land in that section. These men formed the Ohio Company, perhaps because they bought land along the Ohio River.

The Ohio Company sent a young surveyor named Christopher Gist to the new land in the Ohio Valley to see just what kind of land it was. He made a very careful survey.

Gist made several maps of the country and sent these maps and a report of its natural riches to the Ohio Company. It was indeed valuable land, for it contained large forests, rich pasture-lands, and many animals.

The French Claim. When the French heard about this, they became quite angry, for they claimed this land as their own. Years before, La Salle and other French trappers had claimed that land for France. Although they had not settled there, they always claimed it as belonging to France.

The French governor, Celeron (sel-e-ron′), was a venerable old man with gray hair. He wanted to make sure that the French would not lose their claim to this land. He started out from Montreal

356

and went south by the Great Lakes into the lands of the Iroquois, and down along the Ohio River. Do you think this was an easy trip?

As he went along, he buried from place to place lead plates on which was written the French claim to this land. At a tree near each plate, he placed the French emblem.

On his way, Celeron also stopped at the Indian settlements. He made friendly visits with the Indians, in order to be sure that they would help the French in case of war.

In order to be sure of holding the all-important Ohio Valley, the French built a fort a little north of the spot where the Allegheny River meets the Monongahela River (mo-non-ga-he'-la). Many, many buffaloes lived on the plains around this spot. This fort was called by the French word for buffalo, Le Bœuf (le buf).

What the English Did. The English decided that they would fight, if necessary, to hold the Ohio Valley. So, two years later, the Governor of Virginia chose a young man of twenty-one years to carry a very important message to the governor of Fort Le Bœuf. This young man was George Washington, whose brother was a member of the Ohio Company.

Young George deserved the confidence and trust placed in him. He was a very good student. When he was only sixteen years old, he was allowed to help some surveyors on the large estate **357** of Lord Fairfax. This estate was close to Washington's home, Mount Vernon.

At the time he set out for the Ohio Valley, George was a fine-looking young man. He was six feet, two inches tall and well built. His hair was reddish-brown, and his face was sunburned from living in the open air.

On the way to the Ohio River, George, with Christopher Gist and other companions, passed over two mountain ranges. Sometimes they tramped through deep snow with their packs on their backs. At other times, they rode their horses through deep forests. Their bed at night was often the cold ground, with only the sky for a roof. The journey took weeks and weeks.

At Fort Le Bœuf, the French commander received Washington courteously, as a messenger from Governor Dinwiddie of Virginia. The commander read the message, which told the French to leave the Ohio Valley at once, because it was English property.

The French commander then told George Washington that the French had no intentions of leaving the country since it belonged to France. To prove to the English that they meant what they said, the French began to build another fort immediately.

WASHINGTON RETURNS

THE French refusal to give up the Ohio Valley

meant that the English colonists would go to war. There were so many of the Indians on the French side, that the English called this war the French and Indian War. Governor Dinwiddie of Virginia prepared for battle. He had only a handful of poorly trained soldiers, while the French had a powerful army.

Governor Dinwiddie needed help. He sent word to the other English colonies that he needed help. These colonies sent a few soldiers, and then went on fishing, plowing their fields, and building ships, as though nothing happened.

A Fort at the Forks of the Ohio. George Washington was placed in charge of the little Virginia army. He and his men made their way through the wilderness and set to work building a fort.

The place Washington selected was called the "forks of the Ohio," an important spot where the Allegheny and Monongahela Rivers meet to form the Ohio. Whichever nation held this fort could use the Ohio River freely, as a passage to the Mississippi River. For this reason, the spot was also called the Gateway of the West.

Before the fort was finished, the French drove the English away from the spot. The French completed it and called it after their French governor, Duquesne (du-kayne'). This all took place in the year 1754.

War Begins. The English withdrew to a place known as Great Meadows. Here Fort Necessity **359**

was built. It gave little protection, but it was the best they could build at the time.

When the French attacked, the battle lasted one full day. More than fifty English were killed, and there was only a little powder left. Sadly, Washington surrendered to the French, and went back to Virginia. This battle at Fort Necessity was

the first battle that was fought in the French and Indian War. Two years passed before England openly declared war on France, but this war really began in America in 1754.

THE PLAN OF UNION

SOMETHING had to be done in order to get the colonists to work together. A meeting was called at Albany, New York, in 1754. It is known as the Albany Convention. Representatives from Massachusetts, New Hampshire, Rhode Island, New York, Pennsylvania, and Maryland discussed how they might best work together against the French.

One Pennsylvania representative at this meeting was Benjamin Franklin. He said that the colonists must give up their selfish ideas and unite, or they could not defeat the French.

The English Disagree. Franklin proposed a plan in which one government would be made for the thirteen colonies, instead of thirteen governments, working at times against each other. His complete plan was called the *Franklin Plan of Union*.

The representatives thought it was a good idea. They took his plan home to the colonists to see if they agreed. The colonists did not want such a union. They were unwilling to give up the freedom they enjoyed in their own colonies. They were still thinking selfishly. They were not working for the common good of all the English colonies in America. They would not unite.

A Lesson to Learn. The colonists still had a lesson to learn. That lesson was that they had to work together as Americans. They had to stop thinking of themselves as members of separate colonies.

They finally learned this lesson. It is a lesson that we have to remember always. We people of America today must realize that we are all

Americans, no matter what race we belong to, and no matter what our religion is.

Sometimes people today forget that. When that truth is forgotten, we do not act like good Americans. Then we can make our country weak instead of strong.

We must always remember that "in union there is strength."

Keeping Up with Our Vocabulary

emblem	neglected	expelled
surveyor	allegiance	Le Bœuf
	intercolonial	

Things to Do

1. Tell why Fort Duquesne was called by that name.
2. Give a floor talk on the Albany Convention of 1754.
3. On the map, page 352, locate the land between Lake Erie and the Ohio River; the point where the Allegheny and Monongahela Rivers meet in the Ohio Valley.
4. Compare the Spanish, French, and English colonies in 1750.
5. Explain why the English colonies were jealous and selfish.
6. Write a report on the reasons why the Iroquois sided with the English in the intercolonial wars.
7. On a new time-line, write the important dates in the history of all the colonies since 1607.
8. Tell the story of the unkindness and cruelty of the English to the Acadians.
9. Give two reasons why both France and England had some claim to the Ohio Valley.
10. Write a short account of George Washington's early life.

CHAPTER II

UNITED ENGLISHMEN

Looking Over the Chapter. A glance at the map on page 352 will give you a good idea of the way our land was divided in 1750 among three nations.

By 1763, this was changed because of the French and Indian War. At that time, Spain and England claimed the entire continent. France lost its lands in America. England had gained all the land blessed by so many French missionaries, and explored by the French trappers and traders. England's land now stretched from the Atlantic to the Mississippi River.

This great change came about after the French and English colonists waged war against each other.

In this unit you will learn that, while England gained more lands after the French and Indian War, the colonists gained much more in other ways. They learned how to carry on war. They learned, too, how great was the strength of their numbers. Most important of all, they learned their common interests as united Englishmen, united Bearers of Freedom.

Braddock's Campaign. In 1755, before war was yet declared, both England and France sent troops to America. An English general named William Braddock, came with over a thousand well-trained troops.

Braddock had led successfully many forces in Europe. However, he knew nothing of the kind of warfare carried on by the Indians and French in our land. He proudly told his men to form lines of battle. He scattered the colonial soldiers here and there among the ranks of his well-trained soldiers.

George Washington was now one of the colonial officers. He warned the Englishman that his kind of warfare would not succeed in the backwoods warfare of our country. But Braddock thought Washington's advice worthless, and refused to pay any attention to him.

At last General Braddock started from Fort Cumberland in Tennessee. He went through the wilderness towards Fort Duquesne. Before him went a group of men clearing the way for his fine soldiers. This road made Braddock's men famous.

Later on, as our country grew, many pioneers used Braddock's Road in traveling to lands farther west.

Near Fort Duquesne. Washington knew the enemy might be hiding along the trail. He wanted **364** to send scouts to watch for them. But Braddock would not listen. Slowly the soldiers walked in orderly file through the wilderness.

When they were near the fort, a Frenchman stood in the middle of the trail. He raised his right hand. From the right and left of the road came many bullets. But no troops were in sight!

Braddock was learning his lesson. The bullets kept coming. The redcoats were quickly shot down

by the unseen enemy behind bushes, rocks, and trees. Two horses were shot dead underneath George Washington, but he remained unharmed.

Washington Takes Over. When Braddock saw that he was losing, he ordered a retreat. Just at that moment, he was struck in the chest, and wounded seriously. The English forces had lost their leader. At once, Washington's men began **365**

fighting the enemy in true Indian style, from behind rocks, trees, and bushes.

At this point, Washington took control and protected the remaining soldiers as best he could. Washington proved himself a good leader. He became famous throughout the colonies.

Up to this time, France and England were at peace. War was declared by England in 1756. Then England began to send generals to America, but these generals were not the best. The next two years were years of defeat for the British.

France sent her best and bravest general, Montcalm. The victories which the French won gave them much confidence. They went farther and invaded the frontier settlements in the Ohio Valley, Maryland, and Virginia. It looked as if England was going to lose her lands in America.

The Indians sided more with the French because they were victorious, and because they promised them even greater trade and friendship in the future.

THE TURNING OF THE TIDE

THE new prime minister of England, named William Pitt, saw that the colonies were very valuable. He was determined at all costs to save them. He was displeased with the way the English were carrying on the war in America.

Pitt ordered 22,000 soldiers to be sent from

England with the two best generals, Amherst and

Wolfe. In the colonies, an army of 20,000 enlisted to fight under the English flag. Things were different now. Colonists went to war because England wanted them to help.

In the meantime, the French under Montcalm had made wonderful progress, gaining command of Lake George.

Hope for the English. A large number of soldiers under the English General Forbes moved against Fort Duquesne. The French thought it would be easy to defeat Forbes. The French had left only one thousand men in the fort, and Forbes had six thousand men.

Forbes moved very slowly. The French got many Indians to help them. In the end, however, the French had to abandon the fort. Before leaving it, they burned it, so that it would be of no use to the English.

At once, the English began to rebuild the fort. They named it after their great leader, William Pitt. Today, Fort Pitt has gone, but the great city of Pittsburgh stands where Fort Pitt once stood.

Do you think Fort Pitt was important to the English? Give reasons for your answers.

At the time Fort Duquesne fell, there were great victories taking place in the northern colonies. Fort Niagara, Fort Frontenac, and Fort Ticonderoga, all fell into English hands.

The flag of England now waved over all forts west of the Alleghenies. 367

ONLY Canada remained in French hands. Quebec, the chief city in Canada, was well fortified. If that city could be taken, France would be forced to surrender.

Wolfe tried and tried for days to reach the upper part of Quebec, but each time he was driven back. Finally, he came upon a path on this steep

hill. He made up his mind to use this hill to reach Quebec.

Plans were made for the capture of Quebec. In the darkness of night, 27,000 soldiers and sailors went up the St. Lawrence River. A great steep cliff rose from the water's edge.

One dark September night, warships sailed

368 back and forth near Quebec just pretending they

were landing soldiers there. But the real landing was taking place just two miles up the river! Forty-five hundred redcoats formed a single line. They carried packs and guns on their backs. They clung to the pointed rocks as they crawled along.

The first group that finally reached the top captured the French guards. After that it was easier and safer for the other groups of soldiers.

Meeting of the Red and the Blue. At the top of the hill, there were miles and miles of level and grassy land called the *Plains of Abraham*. At dawn the next morning, Montcalm received a surprise. Wolfe was there. He was outside the French barracks. Wolfe was in Quebec!

There was only one way for Montcalm to fight. **369**

He had to fight the English on the Plains. This was true military warfare, for there were no trees or rocks on this level land.

The redcoats stood in ranks. The French in blue coats, also stood in ranks. Soon a bloody battle began.

Montcalm was wounded early in battle. As his loyal soldiers came to his side, he said, "I am happy that I shall not live to see the surrender of Quebec."

Wolfe, too, was wounded, but he continued in battle. Another bullet hit him in the chest, and still a third. His men carried him to the rear line of battle. There, he saw in the distance the redcoats break through the French lines. "God be praised, I die in peace," he said.

Today, in the garden of the governor's residence in Quebec, there is a monument to the memory of these two fallen generals, Montcalm and Wolfe. Each fought bravely. Each gave his life for what he thought was right.

Quebec fell. England won. It happened in 1759.

But the war continued in Europe until 1763, when peace was made. As a result of this war a great many important changes were made in the lands in America.

The following arrangements were made by the treaty of peace in 1763. Study them carefully for they have a great bearing on the future history of our great country.

1. France gave England all of New France and all lands east of the Mississippi River.

2. France gave Spain all the territory west of the Mississippi, and the city of New Orleans.

3. England gave France only fishing rights off Newfoundland and two unfortified rocky islands near Newfoundland.

4. England gave Cuba and the Philippine Islands to Spain.

5. Spain gave Florida to England.

ENGLAND'S CATHOLIC SUBJECTS

The war left a large country with French-speaking people to be ruled by an English King. It also left Protestant England with strong Catholic subjects. These Catholics were wondering about their future religious freedom. The question was settled in 1774, when the English government passed a law called the *Quebec Act*.

The Quebec Act stated that Canada would be governed in the future by English law. The people of Canada would have the freedom to practice their Catholic religion. You will read more about this Quebec Act in LEADERS OF FREEDOM.

The Canadians were happy that they were free to practice their religion. They loved and valued **371** their holy faith. They rejoiced to know that, although they lost their country's flag, yet they had not lost the blessings and comfort of the true faith.

FRUITS OF STRIFE

France's Doom. France learned her great mistake all too late. She had hunted and traded in New France but did not encourage settlements. She wanted wealth from the fur trade. She forgot that living on the land was a far greater claim than forts and trading-posts. With so much land, and so few settlements, it could hardly be well protected.

The English Learn a Lesson. The people of the colonies thought of themselves as Englishmen. They were devoted and true to their beloved England. But, among themselves, they were jealous of one another. This was the case in 1754. They were not united Englishmen, but divided Englishmen.

Benjamin Franklin described the English colonies very well at the Albany Convention of 1754. He showed a picture he had made of a snake divided into thirteen parts. Underneath the picture was written: "Join or Die!" This kind of picture is called a cartoon. It was probably the first cartoon made in the colonies.

Now in 1763, these colonies had fought a war and won it, with the help of England. They began 372 to see that "In union there is strength." After the

French and Indian War, the colonists began to see things differently. Working and fighting together had made them confident of their skill and power in battle. They depended less on England.

The colonists began to feel a new kind of independence. It was an independence that came out of the wealth of land, soil, and climate that was theirs in this new land.

Since 1609, they had made their homes on this continent. By 1763, they had customs and laws of their own. They had products of their own, and songs, and legends. They began to have a greater love for these things of their own, than they had for those of "merrie England" of long ago. They were changing from English colonists to real Americans.

BENJAMIN FRANKLIN did many things to help build up America. We say he is one of the makers of America. He was a printer, writer, publisher, inventor, and statesman. He was always doing something to help other men.

Franklin was born in Boston, the capital city of Massachusetts Bay Colony, in 1706. Before he went to school, he taught himself to read. As his family was not rich, Franklin had to leave school after two years. He worked in his father's candle shop. Young Benjamin did not like this work.

At twelve, Franklin went to work in his brother's printing shop. He quickly learned his trade, and continued his studies at the same time.

When Benjamin was seventeen, he went to Philadelphia. When he got there, he was so hungry that he bought three loaves of bread for a few pennies.

He must have looked very strange, walking down a street in Philadelphia, eating a loaf of bread, with a loaf under each arm. A girl in a doorway laughed at him as he went by. This girl must have changed her mind about him later, for she became Mrs. Benjamin Franklin!

At this time, Franklin began printing *Poor Richard's Almanac,* and continued it every year for twenty-five years. It was found in every colonial home, together with the Bible. In the almanac, **374** he reprinted many sayings which have lasted through the years, such as: "Lost time is never found," and "Whatever is worth doing is worth doing well."

Franklin printed a newspaper called *The Pennsylvania Gazette*. He started the first circulating library in America and the first fire department. Out of his own money, he hired men to sweep the streets and light them at night.

Franklin was also very active in government. He represented Pennsylvania at the Albany Convention and planned the Academy of Philadelphia. Later this academy became the University of Pennsylvania.

In 1753, Franklin proved that lightning is electricity. He invented the first improved heating stove. He also wrote the story of his life.

You will learn more about this outstanding American in your history next year. He stands out prominently in the fight for independence as one of the LEADERS OF FREEDOM.

Our Land. We have seen in this book how our land was discovered and how it grew. We saw that little by little the people of America came to realize that they were Americans.

In our next book, we shall read about how America became a free nation.

This is a land that has been richly blessed by God. He has given us a land where men are free to love Him and worship Him. We are very fortunate.

This is a land which is dedicated to Our Lady. **375**

She will surely watch over us and guide us if we love her and pray to her.

The future of America rests with all of us—boys and girls as well as men and women. We must be strong as well as holy.

Can You Use These Words in Sentences?

common interests	Fort Pitt	rear line
prime minister	military	statesman
barracks	experience	frontier settlements
cartoon	academy	Plains of Abraham
circulating	victorious	monument
backwoods warfare	fortified	almanac

Things to Do

1. On an outline map of North America fill in the important places and important events connected with the French and Indian War.

2. Study the map at page 352. Explain to the class why lands in America changed hands in a short period of time.

3. Tell why the colonists were unwilling to help Virginia secure lands for the Ohio Company, and yet a few years later these same colonists took part in the war.

4. Pretend you were living in New France in 1774. Write a letter to a friend in France telling how you feel about the Quebec Act.

5. Locate in your library more stories about Benjamin Franklin. Bring them to class. Perhaps your

teacher will ask you to make a report of these stories.

6. Whom do you admire, Montcalm or Wolfe?

High Lights of the Unit

Turn to page 347, where the outline of this unit is found. Using this outline for a guide, write at least five sentences, telling the high lights of this unit.

Can You Explain the Importance of Each of the Following?

Pitt	Albany Convention	Ohio Valley
Forbes	Capture of Fort	Fort Duquesne
Wolfe	Duquesne	Quebec
Gist	Fall of Quebec	Acadia
Washington	Cruelty to Acadians	Canada
Franklin	Quebec Act	
Braddock	Braddock's Defeat	

Test Yourself on Dates

Draw a line from top to bottom in the middle of your paper. On this line place the ten most important dates you have learned this year. When completed, compare your answers with those of your classmates. Explain why you consider each date important.

UNIT SIX — MASTERY TEST

I. Number lines on your paper, 1 to 5. Match correctly the names below with the words in the second column:

Washington	prime minister of England
Pitt	victorious at Quebec
Braddock	killed in the Ohio Valley
Montcalm	a young surveyor
Forbes	captured Fort Duquesne

377

II. Continue to number the lines on your paper to 10. Match the dates with the events:

1759	Cabot's explorations
1497	Acadia taken by English
1754	End of Quebec
1713	Quebec Act
1774	Albany Convention

III. Arrange these events on your paper in the order in which they occurred:

  a. The Mayflower Compact was signed
  b. The first French colony in America
  c. The first English colony in America
  d. The establishment of New Netherland
  e. Slavery introduced into the English colonies

Do the same with the following group:

  f. The last English colony founded
  g. England gained Acadia
  h. Fort Duquesne captured by the English
  i. France lost Canada
  j. Braddock is defeated and killed

IV. Complete these sentences on your paper:

  1. The three nations whose people were in North America in 1750 were _____, _____, and _____.

  2. No missionaries came with the English on their expeditions because _____.

  3. Benjamin Franklin suggested a Plan of Union for the colonies at the _____.

  4. Acadia became Nova Scotia after _____ _____ War.

  5. Catholics in Canada were allowed to practice their religion under the famous _____.

  6. The Acadians were driven from their homeland because they refused to _____.

7. France lost all lands in America after the
   _____.

8. The English, under General _____, captured Quebec.

9. The prime minister, _____, sent soldiers to the English colonists.

10. The French claimed territory west of the Alleghenies because _____.

V. Number your paper 1 to 10. Answer the following questions with "Yes" or "No":

   1. Did Washington take charge of the colonial army when Braddock fell?

   2. Was the Quebec Act passed in 1759?

   3. Was Acadia taken by the English after King George's War?

   4. Was Franklin an inventor?

   5. Did the French Catholics receive freedom of religion in 1759?

   6. Was New Orleans given to Spain in 1763?

   7. Did England take Florida in 1713?

   8. Was the battle of Quebec fought behind rocks and bushes?

   9. Is Pittsburgh located at forks of the Ohio?

   10. Did France claim the Ohio Valley because La Salle explored it?

VI. In each group of words below, there is an unnecessary word. Copy the sentences on your paper, omitting the word that does not belong in each sentence.

   1. Pitt was a statesman, farmer, English leader, prime minister.

   2. North America was settled by France, Spain, Portugal, England.

379

3. Acadians were sent to Louisiana, Baltimore, California, New England colonies.

4. Places connected with the French and Indian War are Quebec, Fort Pitt, Florida, Albany.

5. Washington, Gist, Franklin, Montcalm were English colonists.

6. French forts which fell into English hands were Fort Niagara, Fort Fontenac, Fort Ticonderoga, Fort Orange.

7. Washington was a soldier, surveyor, messenger, inventor.

8. The Ohio Valley contained fisheries, good forests, pasture-lands, animals.

9. France lost Canada, the Great Lakes, Virginia, New Orleans.

10. Benjamin Franklin was a printer, baker, writer, statesman.

VII. Answer the following in complete sentences:

1. Who was the first English commander sent to the Ohio Valley?

2. Which Spanish territory became English property in 1763?

3. Give the reasons why the Albany Convention failed.

4. Why did Virginia colonists buy land in the Ohio Valley?

5. Why did the English consider the Ohio Valley theirs?

6. Which country had the greater claim to the Ohio Valley?

7. If you had lived in New Orleans in 1764, would you have been living on French or Spanish soil?

INDEX